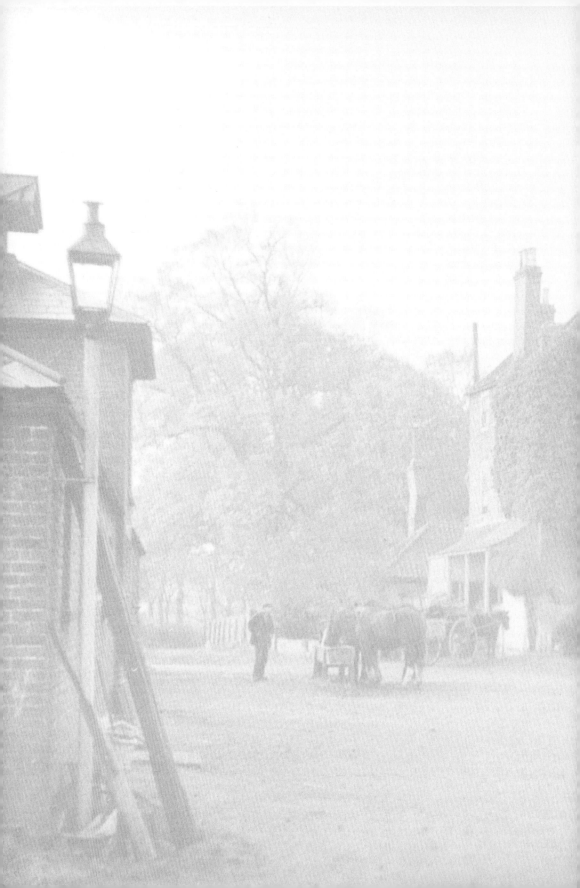

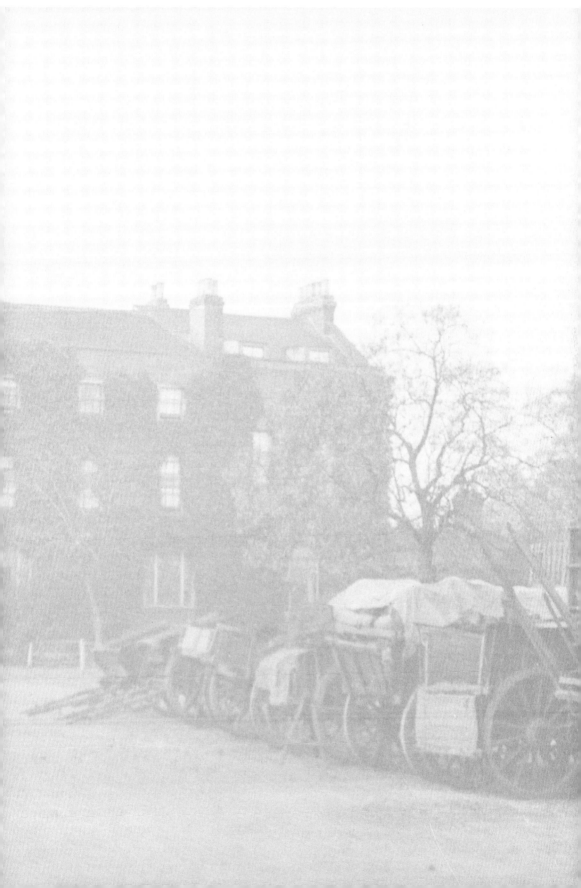

A CENTURY *of*
ILFORD

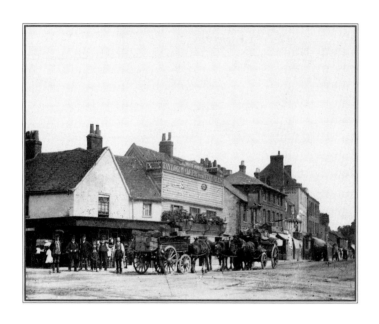

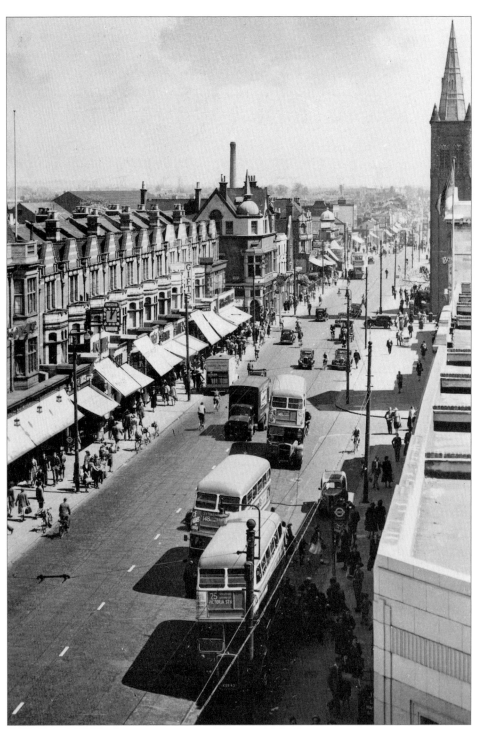

The town along the High Road, *c.* 1950.

A CENTURY of
ILFORD

BRIAN EVANS

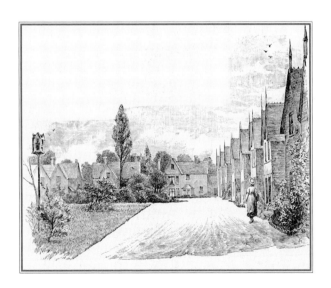

First published in the United Kingdom in 2001 by
Sutton Publishing Limited exclusively

This new paperback edition first published in 2012

The History Press
The Mill, Brimscombe Port
Stroud, Gloucestershire, GL5 2QG
www.thehistorypress.co.uk

British Library Cataloguing in Publication Data
A catalogue record for this book is available from the British Library.

ISBN 978-0-7524-7966-8

Illustrations

Front endpaper: Goodmayes Farm, a substantial house and spacious farmyard with various outbuildings, typical of old rural Ilford. It is shown on maps of the late 1920s with Westrow Gardens to the west and Breamore Road to the north. Tresco Gardens, Brownlea Gardens and Budoch Drive now run across the site.
Back endpaper: The span of a century. On the right are houses from the beginning of the century, with new development in progress on the left. In the middle are the Central Library and the underpass.
Half-title page: The agricultural village, Ilford Broadway, *c.* 1880.
Title page: Before the century began — Dr Barnardo's Homes. Note the birdhouse on the lawn to the left.

Contents

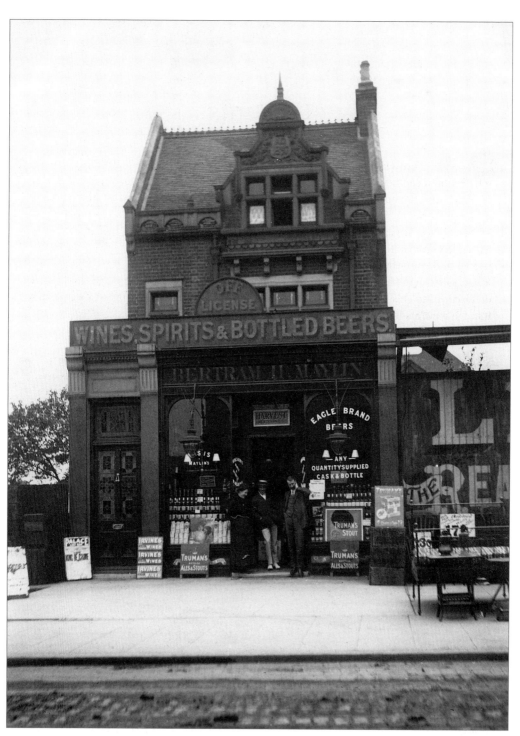

Bertram Henry Maylin's off-licence, No.230 High Road, Ilford, *c.* 1909.

Introduction

The story of Ilford's rise to the status of a premier suburb and regional shopping centre in the twentieth century is a study in contrast between countryside and development. In May 1905 Charles Reynolds recounted how there was enough farming interest in the area to form the Ilford Farmers' Association, which became one of the foremost organisations of its type in East Anglia before the First World War. In 1907 it held its first ploughing match, with thirty-five ploughs competing. The year after there was a much bigger show, including horses, and competitions for corn, fruit and vegetables. As was to be expected, a separate tent was set aside for the ladies, where honey, jam, butter, cakes, eggs and flowers were on display. But this was not all, for there was a straw-tying competition, and stacking and thatching events in which the rivalry was fierce. Contests for the best crops of wheat, oats,

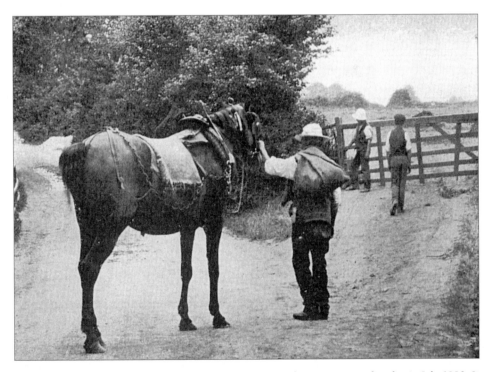

This picturesque view was taken in Water Lane at 5 p.m. in the evening on a fine day in July 1902. It reminds us of the importance of the horse in all everyday activities, especially farming, at the beginning of the twentieth century.

potatoes and cabbages were actually judged *in situ* on the farms. It can readily be seen that at this time the main occupations of Ilfordians were agriculture and the land. As late as 1918 there was still a healthy remnant of the farming land that had originally existed here. In the 1922 *Directory* we still find a considerable number of 'dairymen' listed, which reminds us that at this time there were families living in temporary buildings in areas such as Clayhall, trying to make a living on smallholdings and allotments.

The process of urbanisation and development in the small town had already begun in the nineteenth century. The coming of the railway with its station, conveniently placed near the central crossroads in 1839, led to an increase in the population. A county handbook a few years later described Ilford as 'a large and populous village with good inns and well stocked shops'. The population at the time was 3,742. But it grew and with the growth came problems. This led at the end of the nineteenth century to devolution from Barking, of which it had formerly been a part. From 1888 Ilford's affairs were managed by three overseers, an assistant overseer and a vestry clerk. In 1890, the new parish was made a Local Government District. Finally, four years later, it became an Urban District. Luckily there was some continuity through the upheaval, as Mr E.J. Beal was the first chairman of each of these successive bodies. With the creation of the UDC there was no holding back progress. Within a few short years Ilford had a new town hall (the front part of the building

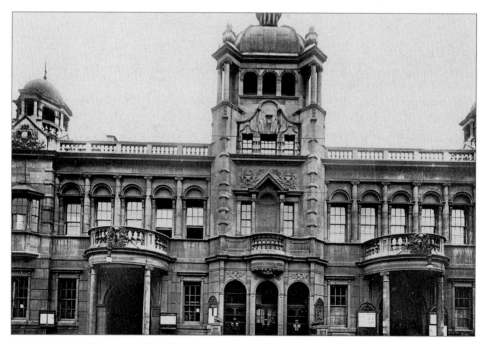

The completion of the town hall in 1901 made the local community feel that Ilford was truly a twentieth-century community, as most towns only had old-fashioned nineteenth-century civic buildings. Designed by B. Woollard, the town hall has been variously described as having 'an ornate renaissance style' and 'in a free classic style'. Enlargements took place in 1927 and 1933. It contains a mayor's parlour with splendid panelling.

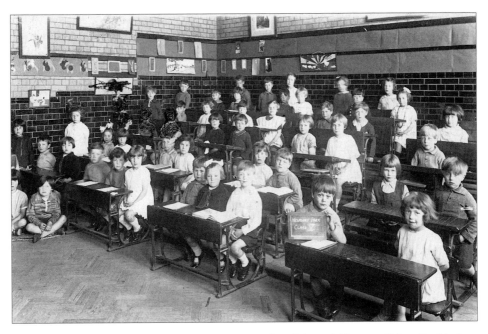

Newbury Park School at the turn of the century. Quite a few of these children would have lived in farm accommodation.

which still stands), as well as an electricity company and a tramway system, both controlled by the local authority. By 1901, the population had risen to 41,229.

'The never failing public well' of 1850 had been replaced by 1901, by the sinking of two new wells. By 1914 the Metropolitan Water Board and South Essex Water Board were supplying all but fifty-three of Ilford's 15,852 households. The village of Ilford had made do with a primitive sewage system until 1893. Population increase dictated that a new system be provided. An arrangement was worked out to convey the sewage by gravitation and pumping to the outfall works in Water Lane, where it underwent treatment. However, within a few years there was an enormous increase in the number of residents in Ilford and the system was deemed inadequate on public health grounds. The Local Government Board was consulted, resulting in the construction of a new sewer flowing to a new outfall on the Thames below the London Northern Outfall Sewer.

The Ilford Gas Company had been operating from an island in the Roding since 1839. In 1899, the new Urban District Council sought to take over the gas undertaking after frequent complaints about high prices. The attempt failed but it did push the gas company into modernising. Thereafter there was tremendous rivalry between it and the council's electricity department, run from a power station in Ley Street which opened in 1901. Through the first half of the twentieth century competition was maintained through advertising and, where possible, by reductions in tariffs.

In 1906, the Homeland Association published the first edition of their *Where to Live Round London* book, which is very complimentary about Ilford: 'There is probably no other London suburb which displays such a wonderful and rapid growth as Ilford. A little more than ten years ago it was a comparatively small place, but today it is a wide-awake go-ahead suburb, equipped with all kinds of modern conveniences, electric tramways, electric light, and one of the finest railway services to the City in existence.

'The area of its business-like local authority contains within its boundaries a population of nearly 65,000.

'The district offers residential accommodation for all classes of the community, and it possesses splendid shopping facilities, whilst the very excellent and complete service of electric tramways, extending in each of the four directions of the compass, place other good marketing centres within easy reach. These tramways also give access to the open country, . . . away to the north and east of Ilford. The area has several fine parks and recreation grounds, the chief of these known as Central Park, containing a lake for boating, swimming and fishing. A beautiful natural park of ten acres has just been presented to the town by Mr Holcombe Ingleby, in memory of his mother.'

The two parks mentioned are now part of Valentines Park, the large extent of which was gradually put together from smaller pieces and included a former farm on the north-east side.

By Forest and Countryside, published for the Great Eastern Railway in 1911, also comments on the suburbs of Seven Kings and Goodmayes at this time: 'These places are

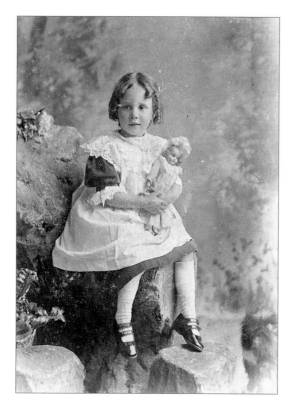

Posing for a photograph in the Edwardian studio of W. Martin in the High Road.

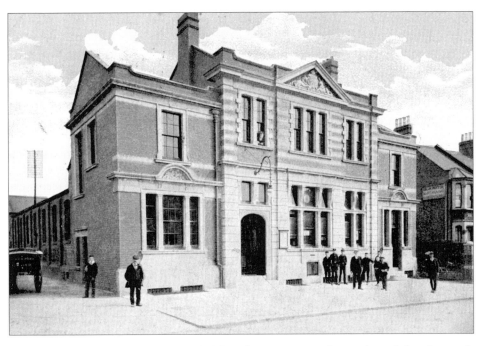

Ilford post office, 1905. Postway Mews is on the left. At this time many people wrote letters daily and postcards were sent in their millions.

mainly the extension of Ilford countrywards. Broad and pleasant roads of comfortable moderate sized houses run north and south from the old Roman highway. The whole area is built on a plain. On the south side the level country stretches down to the Thames and beyond with a pleasant peep at the range of Kentish Hills. Northwards the ground rises gently to Chigwell and what was once the Forest of Hainault.'

'Mainly agricultural country (devoted for the most part to corn growing and the raising of vegetables), borders the residential district; it abounds in footpaths, and many of the country roads are pleasantly margined with grass; and tufted elms, denuded of their lateral branches, standing on the margins of fields are quite characteristic of the district.

'Goodmayes and Seven Kings are within a mile of each other, and in no other place to our knowledge will be found such an assemblage of streets of pleasant houses of moderate size. It may be safely said that nearly all residents at Seven Kings and Goodmayes own their houses, and there is an air of great comfort and display of care about the condition of the many homes with their neat gardens that is very pleasant.'

The last comment may seem strange in these days of widespread home-ownership, but in 1911 and for another fifty years most people rented their properties. In the guide, rental rates per annum are given as £24 to £50 in Seven Kings and £24 to £55 in Goodmayes.

Twentieth-Century 'City'

By 1921 the population of Ilford had reached 85,194. There had, of course, been a slackening of the pace of growth which had been so phenomenal during the first ten years of the century and before. Ilford was busy absorbing the new people, but the death toll of the First World War caused a shortage of male workers. The period of rapid expansion had thrown up remarkably standard streets of houses for the different classes of families. One factor in the move to an Ilford house would have been nearby employment for the working man – many industries then were labour-intensive – so there was a large variety of job opportunities. For the slightly more prosperous, as a large proportion of Ilfordians were, the easy access to London by train threw open the thousands of office vacancies there, and a new breed of independent women began to emerge, becoming stenographers and secretaries in large firms and small. Ilford was setting a twentieth-century trend. It was also ahead in the numbers of schools and colleges available for superior and for commercial education. Then, of course, there were the shops – Ilford became a kind of early Lakeside, the place to visit for 'smart' shops and stores. Many became household names over a large area of East London and Essex.

And at the end of the century the town began reinventing itself with a new road system, new buildings, pedestrianisation and an innovative shopping centre. And at least a few old businesses had survived the century.

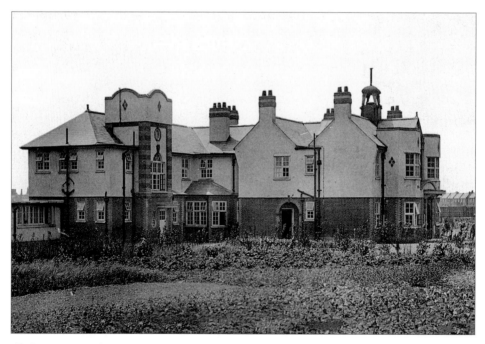

Ilford Cottage Hospital.

Power to the People

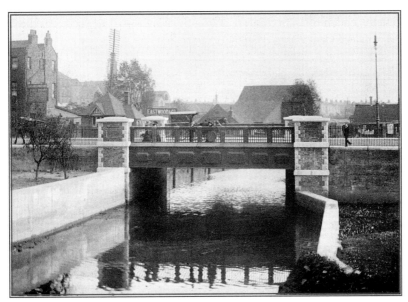

Looking southwards down the Roding from the smart new bridge at Ilford, *c.* 1910. Some of Ilford's industries were located near the river, including the Ilford Gas Company. Ilford photographic works were opened just to the east of the river and Howard's chemical works were also located further south along the river, having moved onto the Lavender Mount area in 1899.

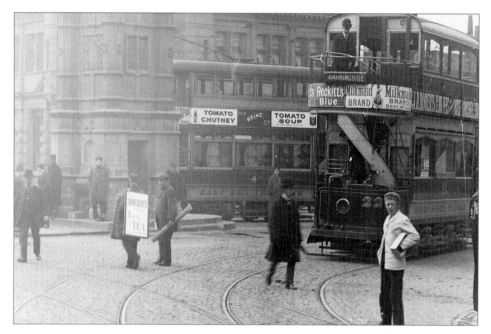

Ilford Corporation tramcar (right) in the middle of the Broadway in 1904. An East Ham car is ready to return towards Manor Park. With few cars on the road the tram was king and even pedestrians and a sandwich-board man could wander about the middle of the highway in a manner impossible at the end of the century.

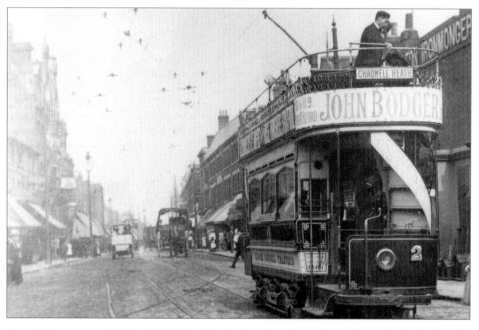

Open-deck tramcar no. 2 in Ilford High Road at the Broadway Junction, waiting to depart for Chadwell Heath, *c.* 1900. Chadwell Heath was the easternmost point of the Metropolitan Essex tramway network.

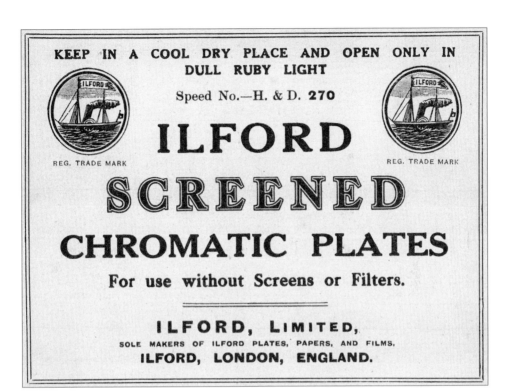

Ilford screened plates. The firm was a pioneer in the development of new film products, first working with and then taking over many other early photographic manufacturers.

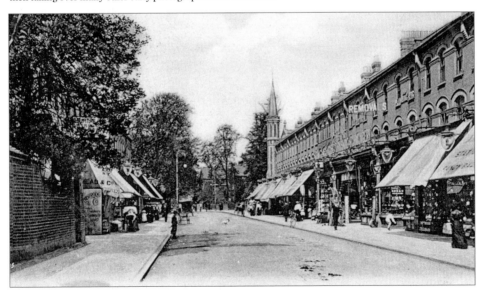

Cranbrook Road, early in the century. On the left is the garden wall of a house, which in the 1920s was the site of an office and shop development. Also visible is the spire of Cranbrook Baptist Church, which suffered war damage in 1940/1 and was replaced by a Tesco store.

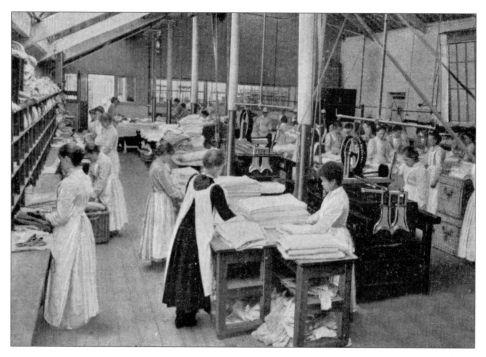

Dr Barnardo's issued this view of the ironing room at the girls' village homes to promote its work during the first decade of the twentieth century.

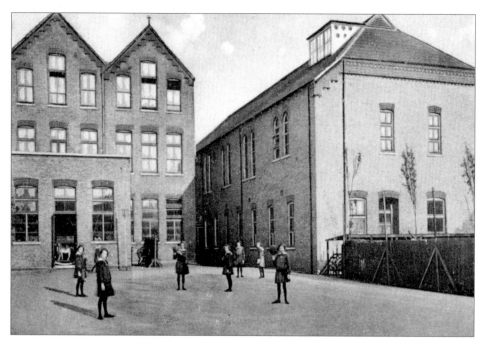

The very solid buildings of the Ursuline High School seen from the playground.

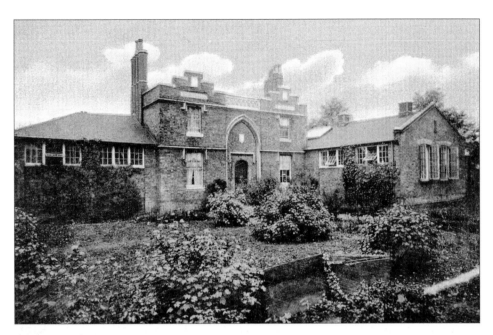

The Church Schools in the High Road, early in the century. They were built in 1830. Part of the school was closed in 1920 and the rest in 1922. Some of the buildings to the east of the church were demolished in 1964 to create an office block.

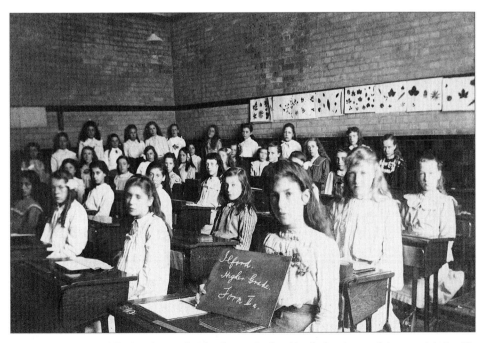

The girls of Form 2a of Ilford Higher Grade School were clearly told to look serious and sit up straight for this photograph. Deportment was actively taught to young girls in the early 1900s.

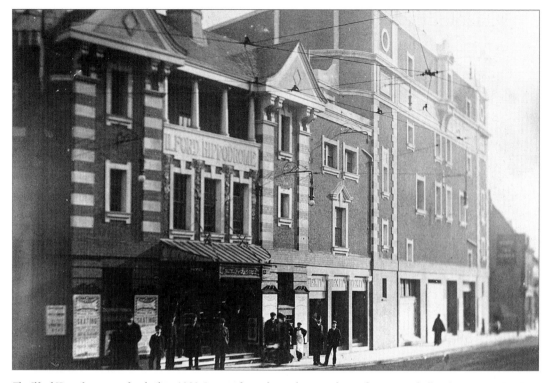

The Ilford Hippodrome was first built in 1909. It opened as a theatre but was also used as a music hall and a cinema. The Black Horse pub now stands on the site.

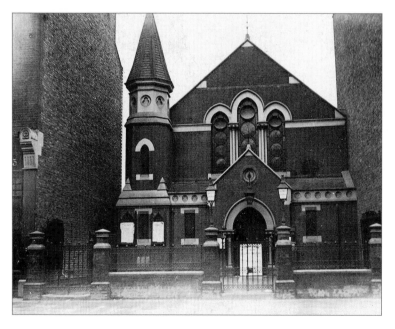

The Baptist Church, 1906. This once stood in the High Road among the shops and like the other churches in the town created a strong community life among its members.

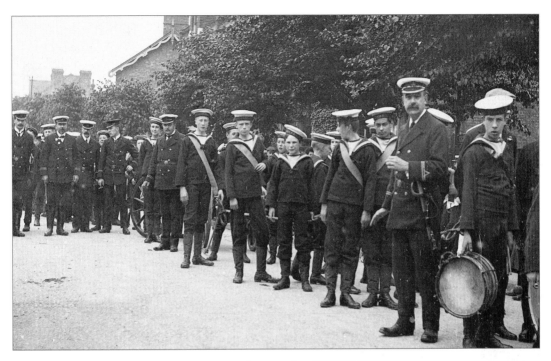

The sea cadets form up, waiting to take their place in the Hospital Carnival procession, 11 July 1908.

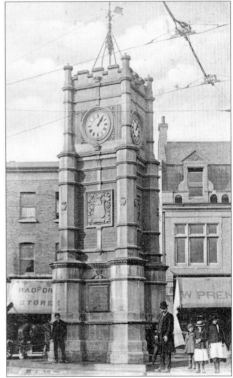

The clock tower, *c.* 1902. 'Meet you opposite the clock tower' was a familiar remark in the early decades of the twentieth century. The tower eventually obstructed tramway improvements and was moved to the entrance of South Park in 1923. This Portland stone edifice was a gift to the town from Cllr W.P. Griggs (later Sir Peter).

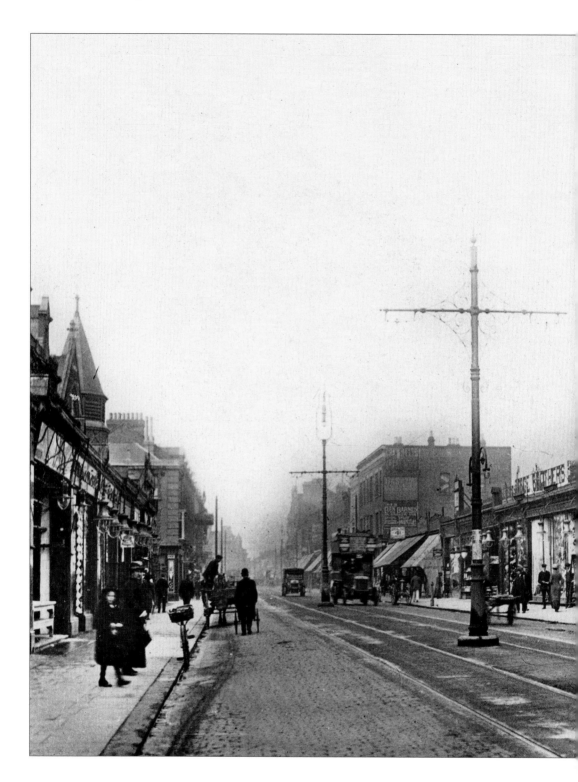

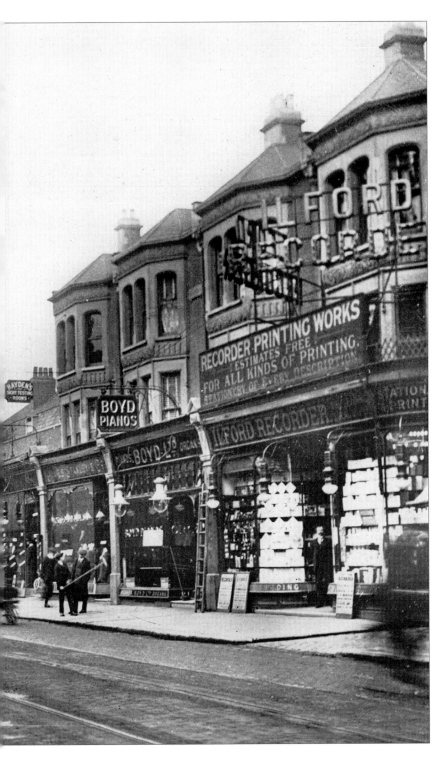

The fine shopping centre of Ilford on the High Road at the beginning of the twentieth century. The Recorder Offices at right – the buildings of which still stand – offer estimates for all kinds of printing. The early bus, with the unreliable steering of those days, is negotiating a path through the rather dangerous tramway poles down the middle of the road. These had to be replaced with a double set, one on either side of the road.

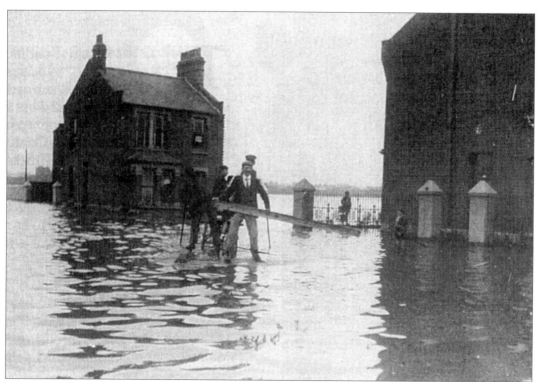

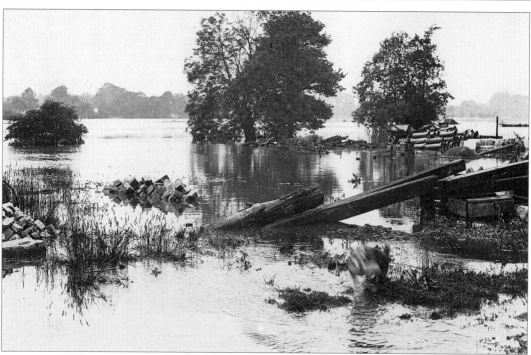

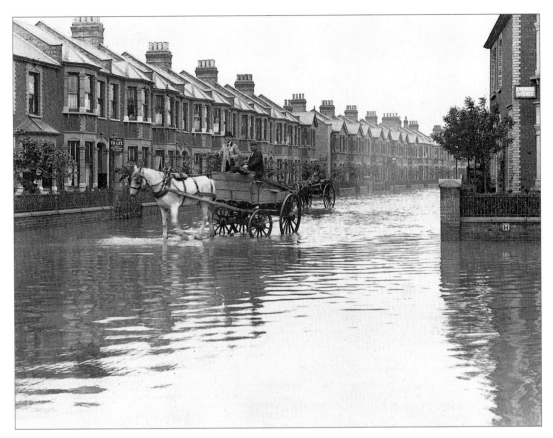

The Ilford floods of 1903 saw the Roding seriously burst its banks. Though some of the floodplain was still open ground, many houses were affected, notably in Wanstead Park Road and Empress Avenue. Some businessmen took a horse and cart instead of walking to the station. Parts of the railway line were inundated and Ilford Lane and Wanstead Park (opposite) were also affected, along with Seven Kings and Manor Park.

Opposite: Flooding has affected the riverside areas of Ilford from time to time during the century, as these 1903 photographs demonstrate.

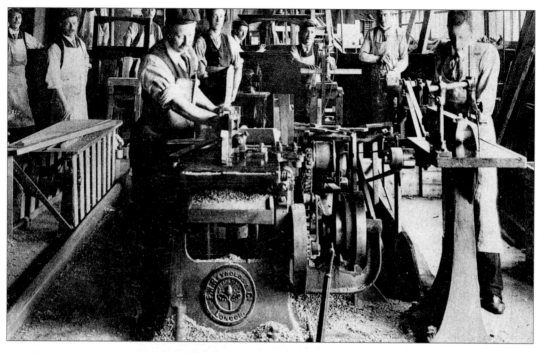

One of the new electrically fitted workshops in Ilford, *c.* 1910. This is S. White's shop-fitting works in Ilford Lane.

ELECTRIC LIGHT

Should be used by all who desire the best and
most economical light FOR ANY PURPOSE.

The price of Current for Lighting Purposes has now been reduced to **4d.** PER UNIT.

On receipt of a Post Card or Telephone Message the Council's representative will gladly call to give advice with regard to the best method of lighting in any particular case.

For Application Forms and further particulars, Address
The ELECTRICAL ENGINEER,
Ilford Council's Electricity Works,
ILFORD.

Telephone No. 32 Ilford.

Ilford Council's electricity department in Ley Street, next to the tramway depot, advertising its services in 1906. Many people used the older gas light system in their homes at this time. Each of the fragile gas mantles had to be lit one by one at night and the light was less strong than that given out by the newer electric system.

Early Suburbs

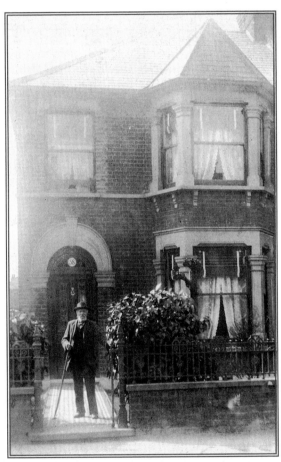

Number 58 Park Road, Ilford, just off the beginning of Green Lane. This was one of the earliest suburbs of Ilford, built over farmland in the early nineteenth century. Grandfather stands at the gate. This house has all the appointments of the typical Victorian/Edwardian home. The venetian blinds hang at the top of the windows in front of the curtains. More privacy is obtained by the front railings, almost certainly removed for the war effort in the 1940s. The path is laid with black and white tiles. It seems that our forebears did not notice how much free light they were blocking out of their homes.

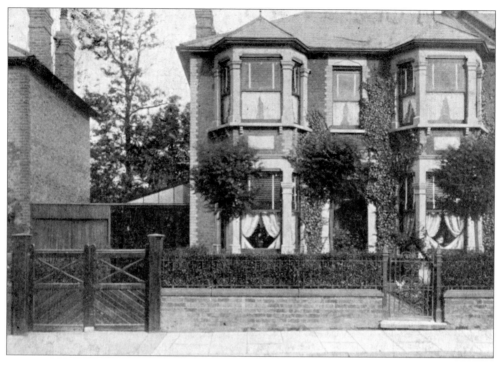

A Cranbrook 'double-fronted' house, 1904.

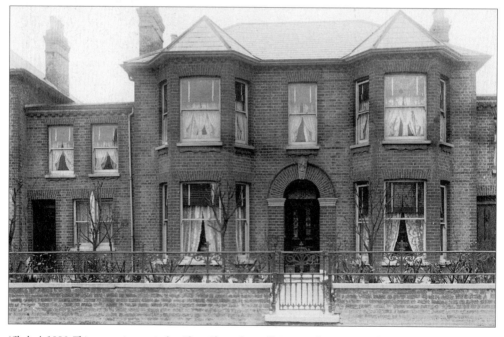

'Chelco', 1906. This was an impressively wide residence, but sadly its exact location is not known.

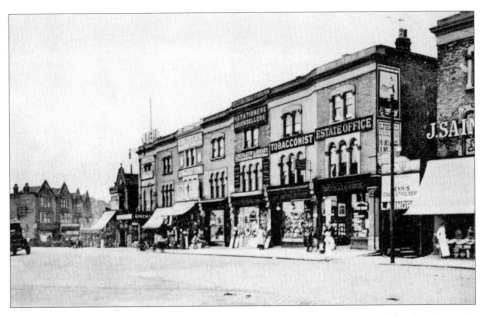

The flourishing shopping and service centre on the High Road, past Seven Kings station. The shopping centre was almost self-sufficient and the transport facilities to other areas were excellent. Note the laundry entrance leading to the mews behind; there was a public hall in the mews at a later date. There was also a cinema here.

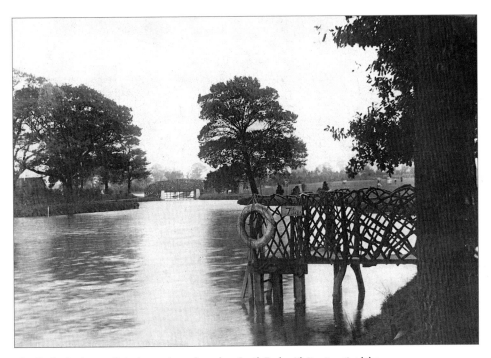

The Ilford suburbs usually had a nearby park, such as South Park with its attractive lake.

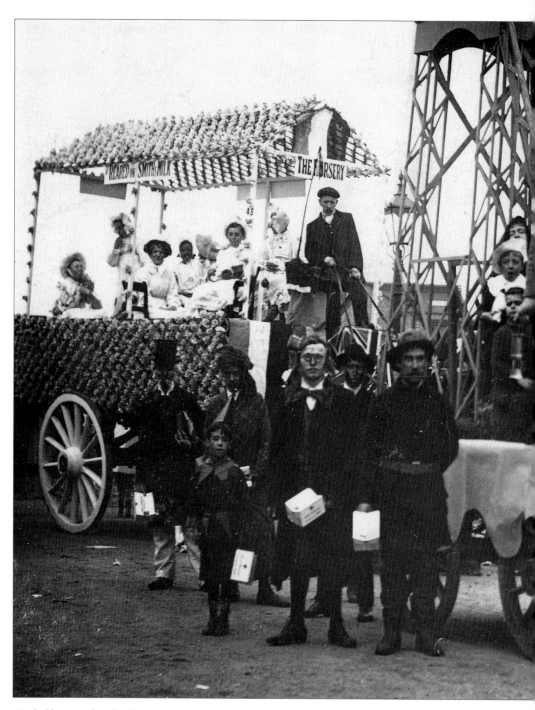

People felt tremendous loyalty towards their area's carnival float. Here, the residents of Loxford Ward have brought a certain working-class solidarity to their theme of 'Everyday Heroes' in the carnival of 1910. This postcard was sent to a soldier serving in the Royal Horse Artillery in the Transvaal, South Africa, in 1910.

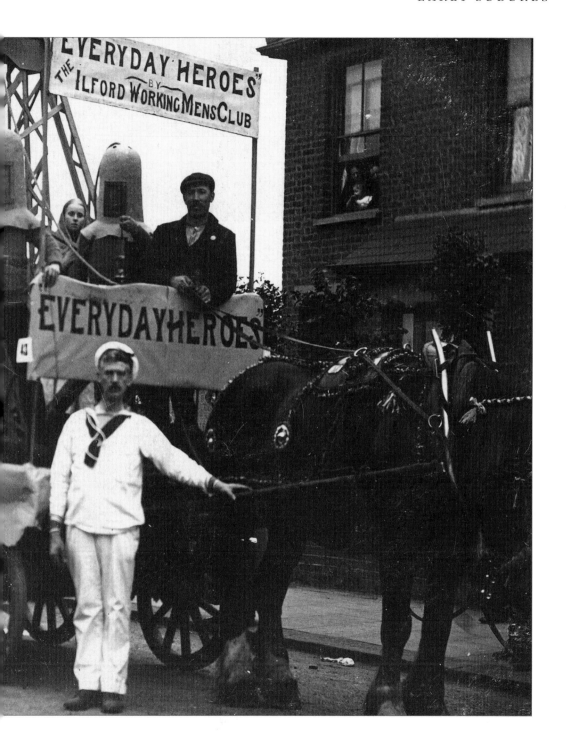

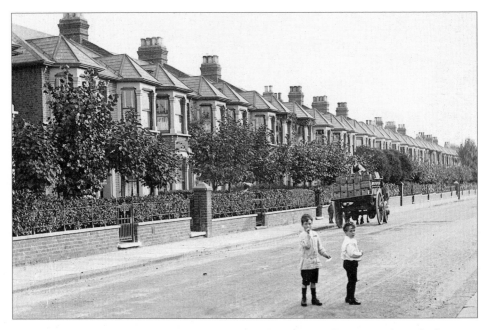

Peaceful Norfolk Road, Seven Kings, in 1907. The houses all have the usual protection of trees, bushes, gates and railings and so on. The horse-cart is loaded with wooden boxes, probably containing ginger beer or beer, or perhaps market garden produce.

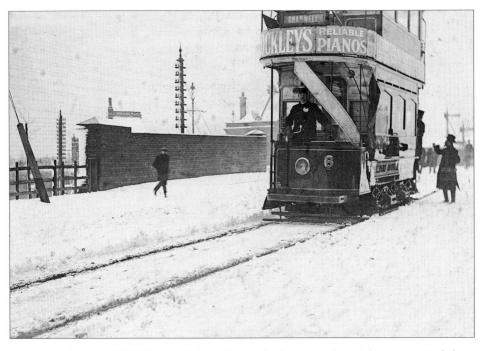

In the bleak mid-winter of 1906. The tram by Seven Kings station bridge provides a vital communication link.

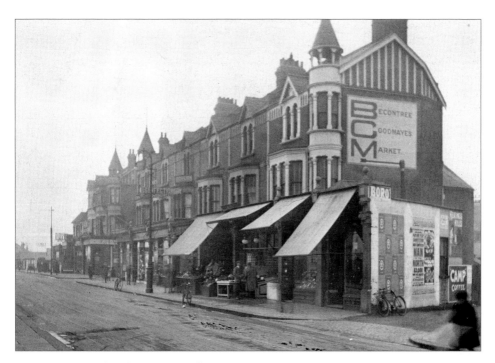

A prosperous row of shops lines Station Road, Goodmayes. Unlike many earlier and later housing developments the Ilford suburbs were provided with shopping terraces from the outset.

In the Olden Time

when Ilford was a small country village, standing amid the fields, there was scanty housing accommodation for the middle classes. The houses were **picturesque but uncomfortable**, few in number and but slightly built.

TO-DAY there is ample choice on

THE CORBETT ESTATES

of well-built Modern Residences, fitted with all up-to-date improvements, and situated in the most healthy part of Ilford.

The MAYFIELD ESTATE Comprising 330 ACRES,

adjoins the Goodmayes Station of the G.E.R., being only 23 minutes from Liverpool-street, to which there is an excellent service of fast trains. Electric Tramways to Ilford Broadway.

By an Easy System of Purchase, persons of moderate means may become **Owners of their own Houses**, which can be obtained Freehold, or on 999 years' lease.

NO Law Charges. **Expenses for Road Making.**

The price of Single Fronted Houses is from £222, and Double Fronted Residences from £314.

Full particulars, with details of the Ilford District Council's loans under the Small Dwellings Acquisition Act, may be obtained on application to

**DAVID BOYD,
Corbett Estate Offices,
Goodmayes,**

Telephone : 50 ILFORD. (Opposite Station).

A Corbett Estates advertisement for the Mayfield Estate which the shops seen above served, 1906.

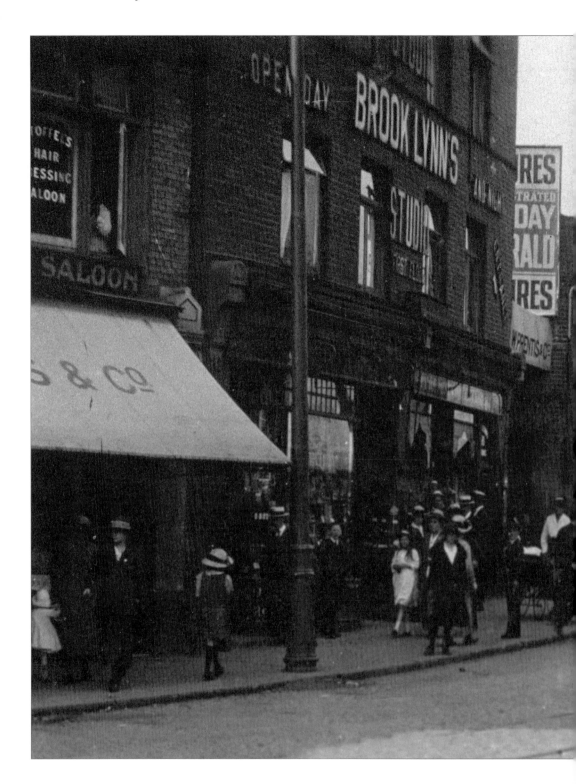

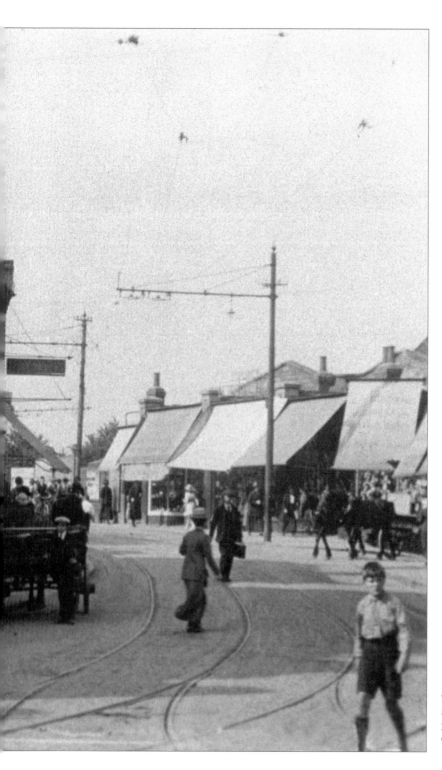

The Broadway, already
a busy place in the early
years of the twentieth
century.

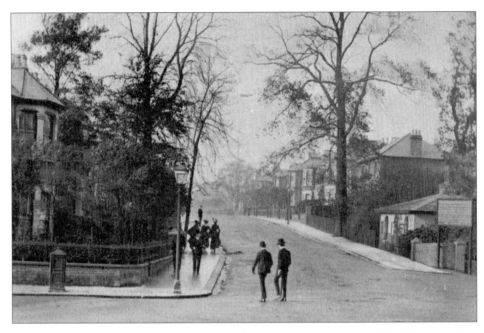

The Drive, at the entrance to the Cranbrook Park estate, 1905. Some of the old trees and the lodge survive from earlier days. The tramway junction box is a symbol of Ilford's new electric era.

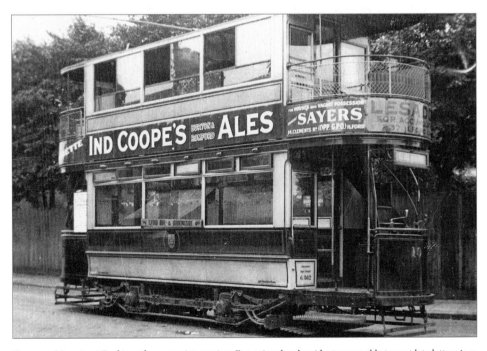

Tram no. 10 waits at Barkingside on a quiet evening. For a time local residents were able to post late letters in a box attached to the tram, which then took the mail back to Ilford to save postmen the journey.

Fight to the Finish

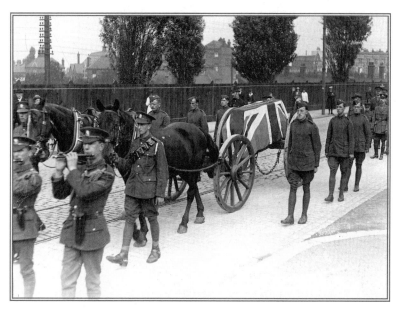

The sad procession accompanying the body of Lieutenant Evans of Norfolk Road on his last journey. Apparently killed on his first flight, his loss epitomises the appalling waste of life in the First World War. Note the style of the airmen's uniform which contrasts with that of the army men. In the background is Seven Kings station and the shopping parade. Hainault Farm airfield was used by Royal Flying Corps in the First World War. Flying was still a very new science and inevitably some paid for their inexperience with their lives before they could see real action against the enemy.

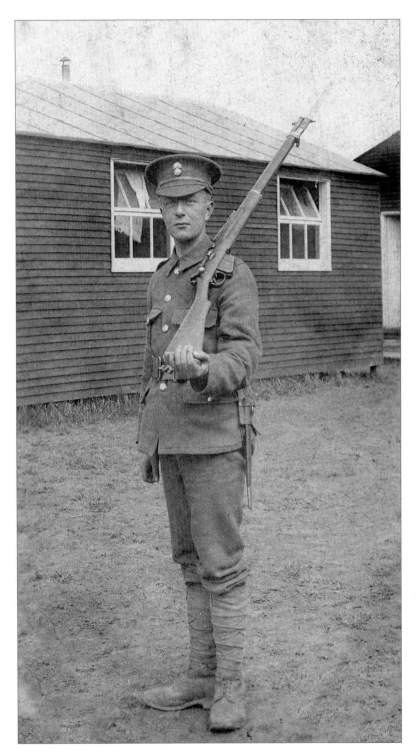

It is believed this soldier had his photograph taken at one of the camps hastily erected in the Ilford area at the beginning of the conflict to hold recruits before they were fully trained and sent to France or Belgium. The photographer J.M. Flatan appears to have made a speciality of taking pictures of service personnel from his base at No.88 Ley Street.

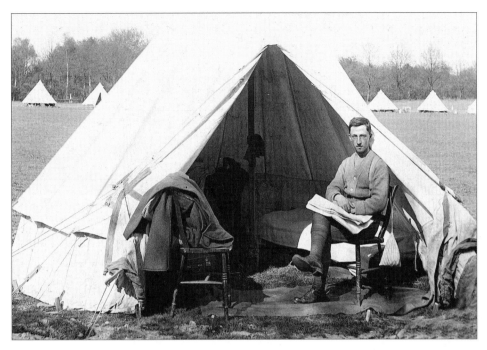

A soldier under canvas, also photographed by Flatau (*sic*), who was now based at No.216 Wellesley Road.

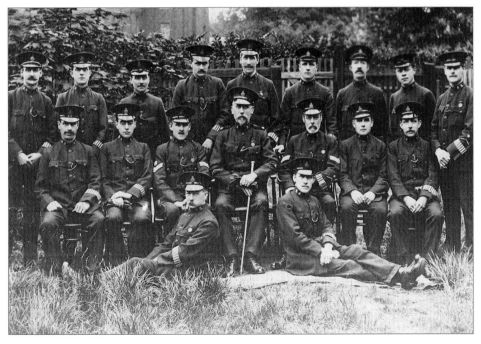

Section 1 Squad 2, the Metropolitan Special Constabulary, Ilford, 1919.

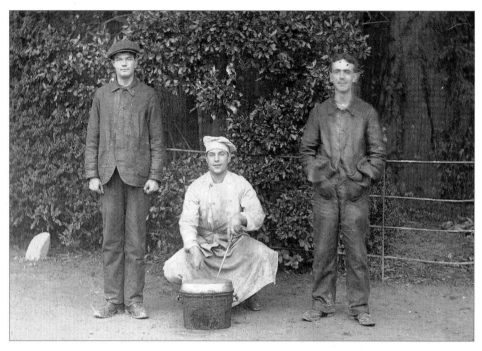

Experiments in emergency camp cooking, possibly in Valentines Park, 12 March 1916. This photograph was taken by the Brook Lynn Studios, No.93 The Broadway, Ilford.

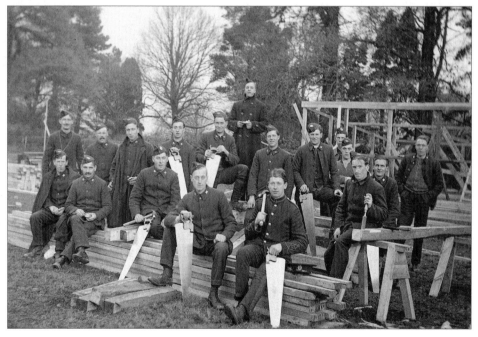

Soldiers engaged in construction work, also photographed by the Brook Lynn Studios.

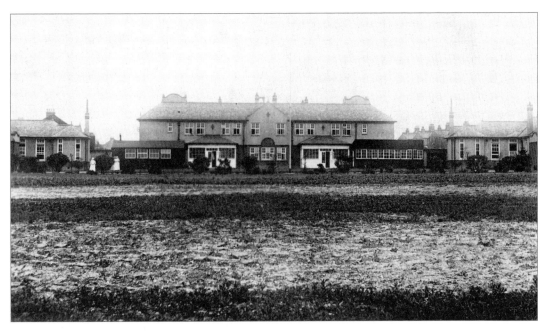

Ilford Emergency Hospital in Newbury Park was opened in 1912 and during the war it had to deal with large numbers of wounded soldiers and other casualties of the conflict.

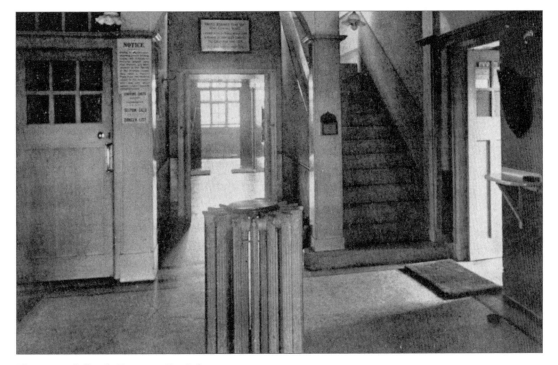

The entrance hall at the Emergency Hospital.

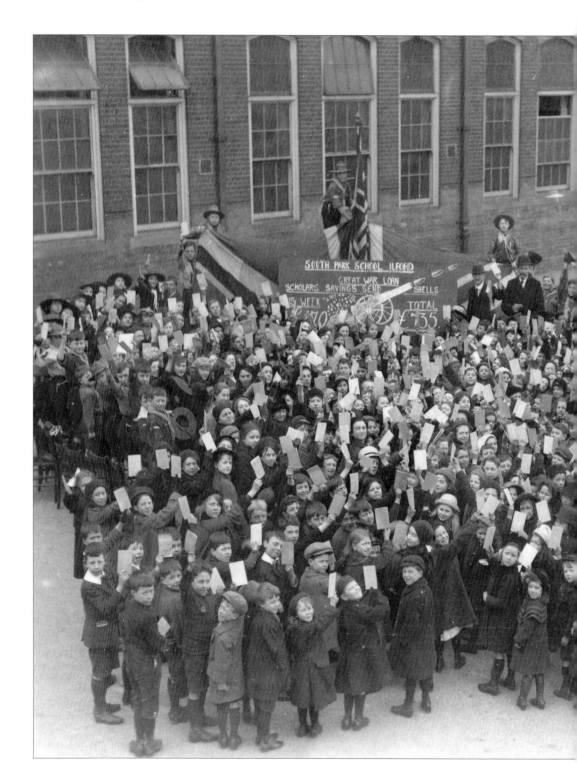

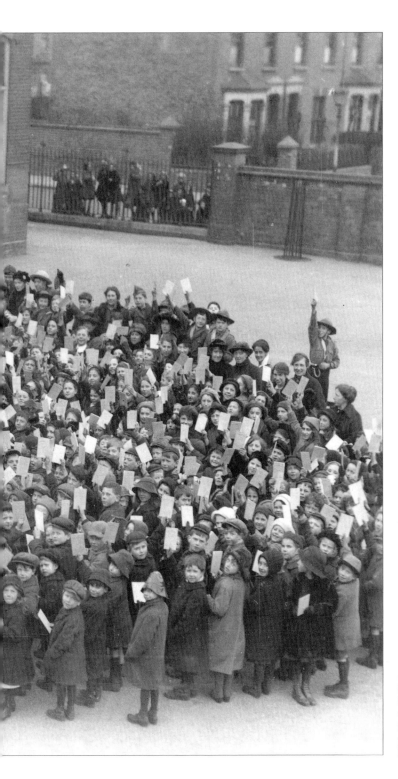

An amazing picture of South Park
School pupils in the playground,
holding up their War Savings
Certificates in 1917. It would be
interesting to know where the
photographer was standing when
he took this shot.

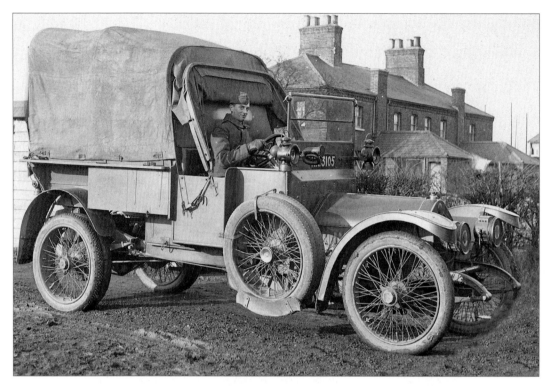

A military vehicle in a field on the edge of Ilford, again photographed by J.M. Flatan, who seems to have been operating in Ilford only during the war period. It seems that the extra activity in the area at this time gave photographers new opportunities over and above those of a busy and populous suburb. Before and after the war, there were more than enough well-established local cameramen in business to supply everyday needs but the unusual conditions of wartime gave enterprising photographers a chance to make their fortunes. And it wasn't just photographers. John Smith (later Sir John), who supplied tents and camping necessities to the army, had never faced such a demand before.

Bright Young Things

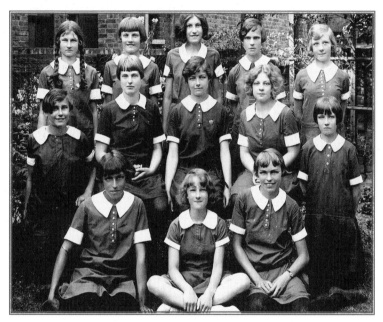

A bright future in store? The twentieth century seems promising for the netball team of St Helen's College in Aldbrough Road, Seven Kings, in 1930. Some of these girls went on to find their true vocation in the Second World War, when changing circumstances gave women more opportunities to work and greater personal freedom. At the secret decoding centre at Bletchley Park in particular women at last got the opportunity to display their real talents.

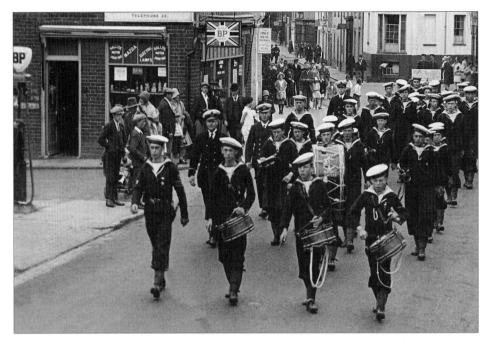

Ilford naval cadets parade through a southern naval town in the 1920s.

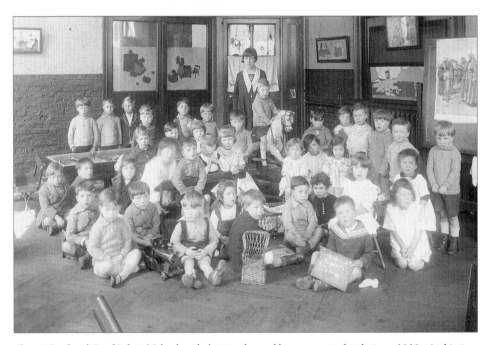

Class 6, Cranbrook Road Infants' School, with their teacher and her very up-to-date haircut, 1920s. At this time many women chose to adopt a more boyish look. Notice the introduction of some toys into the classroom. Mixed classes of boys and girls were becoming more common.

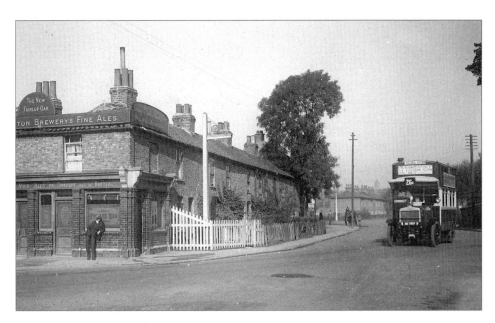

An early motor bus on route 26a makes its way past Britannia Cottages and the New Fairlop Oak in the 1920s. One man appears desperate for the doors to open at the 'Oak'.

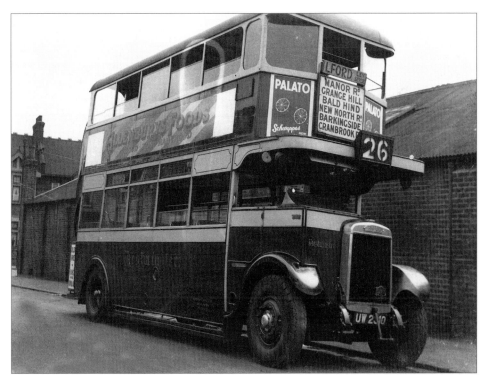

An 'independent' bus, run by the Westminster company, waits in Thorold Road, Ilford, on route 26.

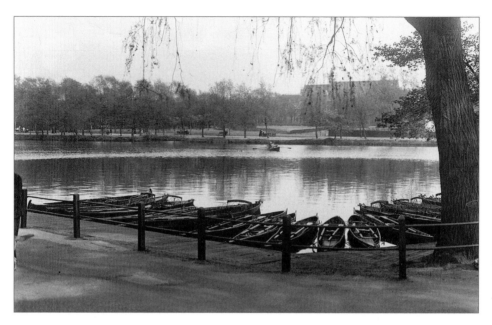

The boating lake in Valentines Park, a place where children and adults could spend many happy hours during the school holidays. Lacking the huge range of amusements now available, many children created a whole imaginary world to live in, undisturbed by today's constant noise and distraction (as visualised in Keith Waterhouse's books about his childhood and his later teenage fantasy *Billy Liar*).

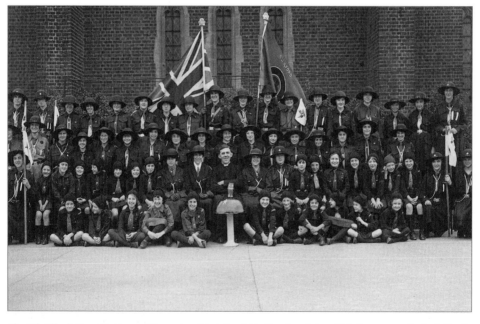

The 6th (Ilford) Essex Guides and Brownies pictured outside the church to which they were attached. Youth groups of this type exerted a strong attraction for youngsters of the time with their relatively inexpensive organised activities.

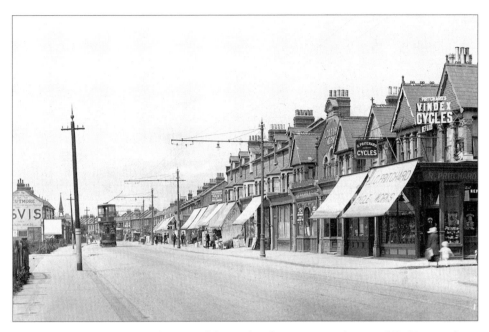

A study in contrasts. The trams and terraces of shops and works premises give this view of Ilford Lane an almost northern-industrial-town air.

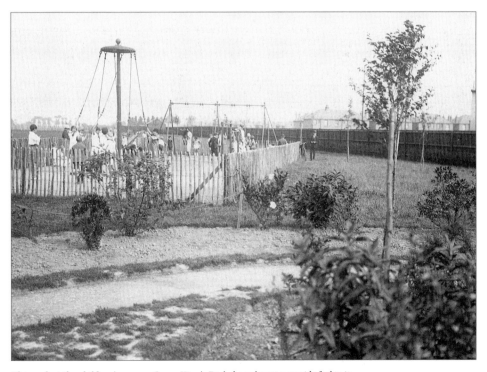

This peek at the children's corner, Seven King's Park, has almost a seaside feel to it.

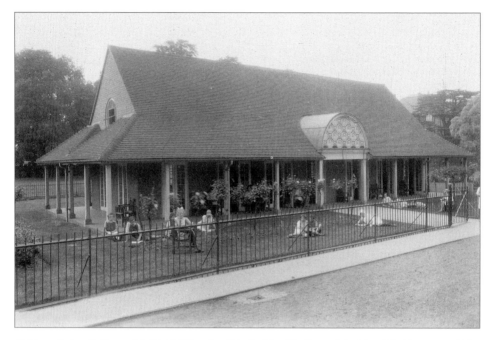

Children at play, Dr Barnardo's Model Village for Girls, Barkingside. Barnardo's claimed that it supported 'the largest family in the world – 8,300 children – over 113,000 admitted'. These figures were updated regularly on the charity's literature, including postcards such as this one.

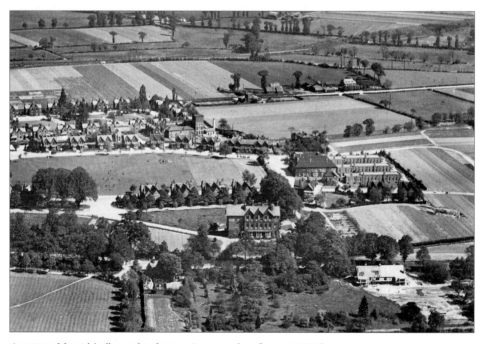

A portion of the girls' village, taken from an Airco aeroplane flying at 1,000ft.

Ilford was becoming one of the busiest suburbs and its stations are included on this railway map showing the start of the old 'Ilford loop', involving a triangular junction between Ilford and Seven Kings. Trains travelled round this loop railway in both directions in the old steam days. After the war the triangle was removed and Newbury Park became an underground railway station accessed by a new tunnel from Leytonstone, with Gants Hill as an extra station in the tunnel. All the old LNER stations as far as Ongar were transferred to London Underground.

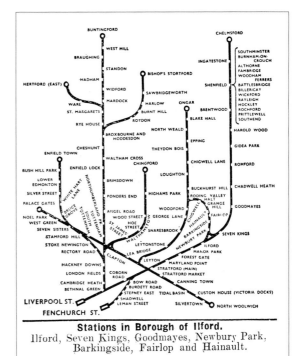

Stations in Borough of Ilford.
Ilford, Seven Kings, Goodmayes, Newbury Park, Barkingside, Fairlop and Hainault.

S. Rowan Heather sits at his desk at the Ilford branch of Mark Liell house auctioneers, July 1929. The house-selling business was booming at this time.

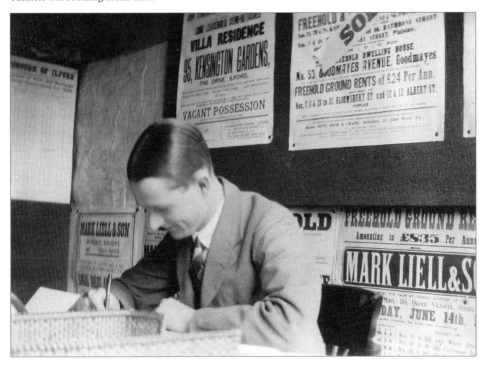

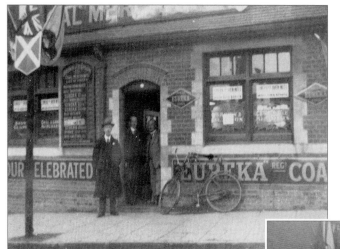

The day at last came when Ilford was to receive its Borough Charter from the Duke and Duchess of York. These two pictures, taken at 9 a.m. and 2 p.m on 21 October 1926, show staff members and the crowd beginning to gather outside the Eureka coal office next to Ilford station.

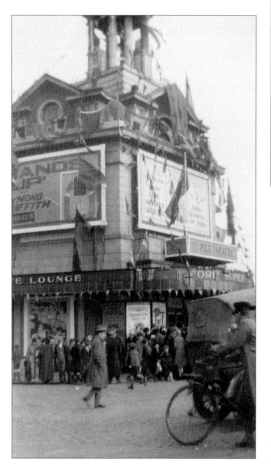

Crowds waiting outside the Super Cinema, which the duke and duchess would visit at 2 p.m.

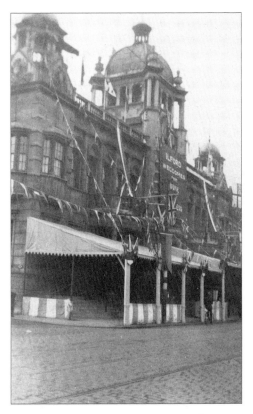

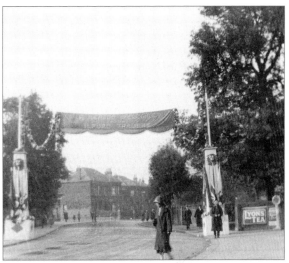

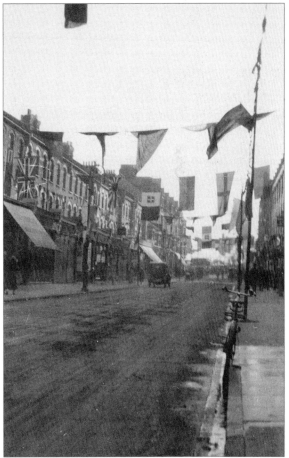

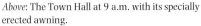

Above: The Town Hall at 9 a.m. with its specially erected awning.

Right, top: The arch put up by the traders at the bend in Cranbrook Road.

Right, bottom: Cranbrook Road mid-street bunting at 2 p.m. The tide of people has washed down to the end of the street to see the Duke and Duchess of York at the Super Cinema.

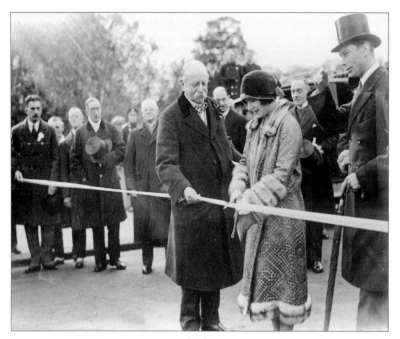

Left: At the boundary of the new borough at Redbridge. Lord Lambourne steadies the tape for the Duchess of York to cut with the ceremonial scissors. Later the duke (afterwards King George VI) was to present the charter officially making Ilford a borough.

Below: Cranbrook Road, and space is getting short. The landmark building on the right corner does not yet have its clock (*see* page 101), which was still in position at the end of the century. Three important concerns are in occupation. On the ground floor is the National Provincial Bank, on the first floor is Randalls, the well-known Ilford estate agents, and on the second floor is the Royal London Insurance Company.

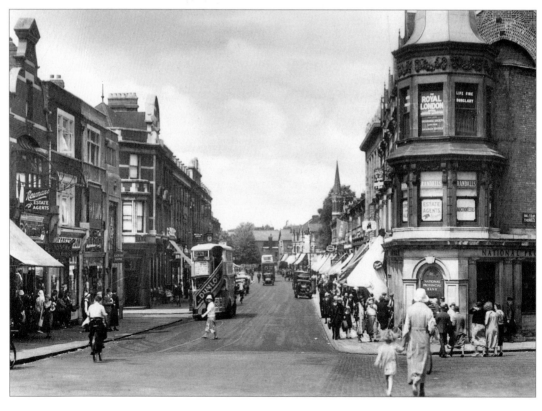

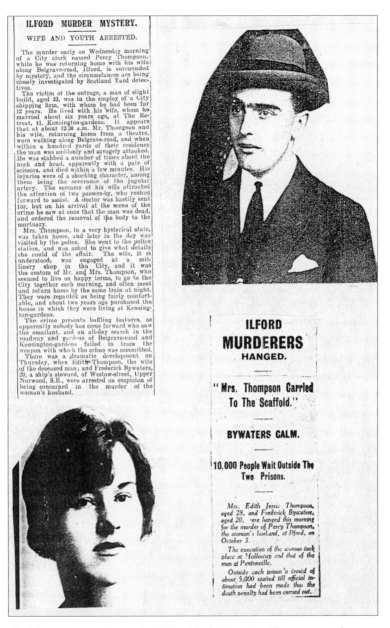

ILFORD MURDER MYSTERY.

WIFE AND YOUTH ARRESTED.

The murder early on Wednesday morning of a City clerk named Percy Thompson, while he was returning home with his wife along Belgrave-road, Ilford, is surrounded by mystery, and the circumstances are being closely investigated by Scotland Yard detectives.

The victim of the outrage, a man of slight build, aged 33, was in the employ of a City shipping firm, with whom he had been for 12 years. He lived with his wife, whom he married about six years ago, at The Retreat, 41, Kensington-gardens. It appears that at about 12.30 a.m. Mr. Thompson and his wife, returning home from a theatre, were walking along Belgrave-road, and when within a hundred yards of their residence the man was suddenly and savagely attacked. He was stabbed a number of times about the neck and head, apparently with a pair of scissors, and died within a few minutes. His injuries were of a shocking character, among them being the severance of the jugular artery. The screams of his wife attracted the attention of two passers-by, who rushed forward to assist. A doctor was hastily sent for, but on his arrival at the scene of the crime he saw at once that the man was dead, and ordered the removal of the body to the mortuary.

Mrs. Thompson, in a very hysterical state, was taken home, and later in the day was visited by the police. She went to the police station, and was asked to give what details she could of the affair. The wife, it is understood, was engaged at a millinery shop in the City, and it was the custom of Mr. and Mrs. Thompson, who seemed to live on happy terms, to go to the City together each morning, and often meet and return home by the same train at night. They were regarded as being fairly comfortable, and about two years ago purchased the house in which they were living at Kensington-gardens.

The crime presents baffling features, as apparently nobody has come forward who saw the assailant, and an all-day search in the roadway and gardens of Belgrave-road and Kensington-gardens failed to trace the weapon with which the crime was committed. There was a dramatic development on Thursday, when Edith Thompson, the wife of the deceased man; and Frederick Bywaters, 20, a ship's steward, of Westow-street, Upper Norwood, S.E., were arrested on suspicion of being concerned in the murder of the woman's husband.

ILFORD
MURDERERS
HANGED.

"Mrs. Thompson Carried To The Scaffold."

BYWATERS CALM.

10,000 People Wait Outside The Two Prisons.

Mrs. Edith Jessie Thompson, aged 28, and Frederick Bywaters, aged 20, were hanged this morning for the murder of Percy Thompson, the woman's husband, at Ilford, on October 3.

The execution of the woman took place at Holloway and that of the man at Pentonville.

Outside each prison a crowd of about 5,000 waited till official intimation had been made that the death penalty had been carried out.

Ilford leapt into prominence in 1922 with the Bywaters/Thompson murder case. The Thompsons, Edith and Percy, had lived at No.41 Kensington Gardens since July 1920. They caught the train to London every day and walked home again from the station every evening, just like thousands of other commuters. The Thompsons formed a friendship with a young sailor called Freddy Bywaters. But Edith and Freddy had a secret love affair and one night, as the Thompsons returned home after a visit to a West End theatre, Percy was stabbed and died. The lovers were both implicated in the crime and both were hanged, though Edith's guilt remains in doubt. Pictured are Ethel Thompson and Freddy Bywaters.

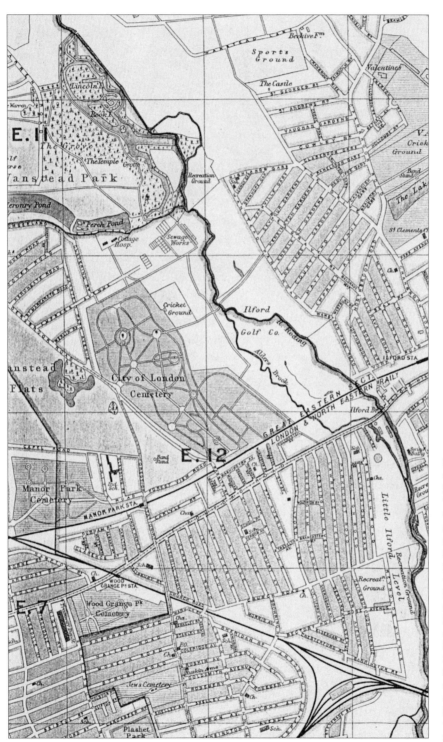

Street plan of
Central Ilford and
its environs, 1925.
The population
was about to leap
upwards again after
a decade's hiatus
from 1911 to 1921.
By 1931, the census
was recording an
increase of 45,852
on 1921's total. The
figure in 1921 was
85,194 and in 1931
it was 131,046. This
meant that more
streets were soon to
appear on the blank
areas of the map.
Seven Kings Park
would fill in the top
north-east corner.

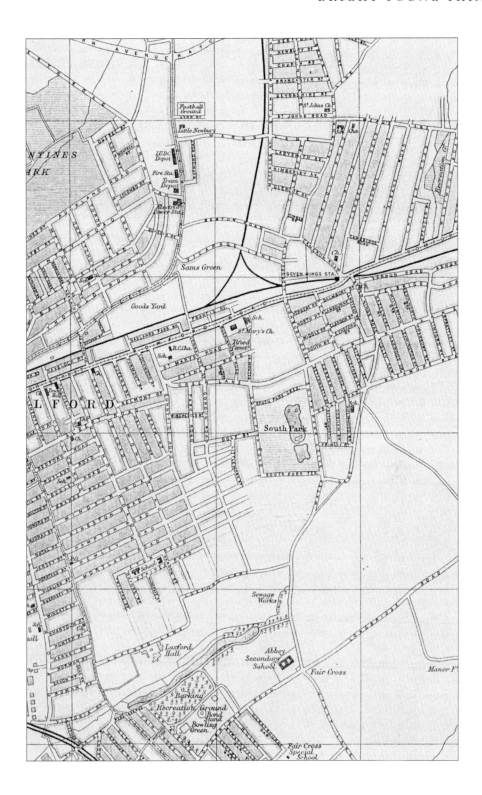

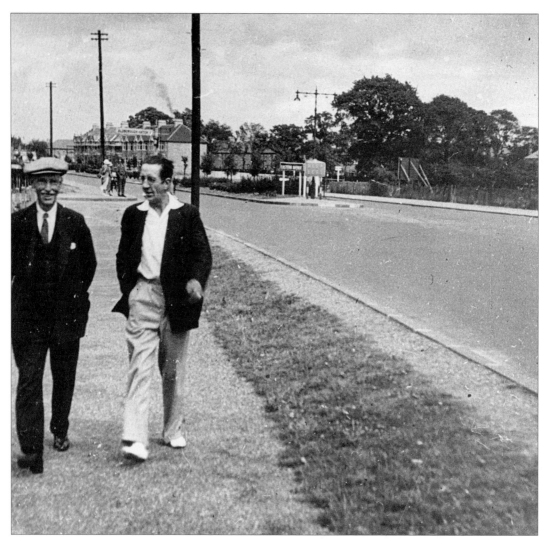

A stroll along Eastern Avenue, newly built and still free from fumes. Just behind the two walkers is a direction post for Aldborough Hatch. For some time after its opening in 1925 traffic was very sparse during much of the week.

A Shrinking World

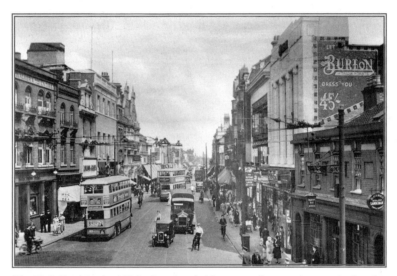

The High Road in the 1930s. In spite of rising unemployment in some trades, the prosperity of the area had gradually increased. The benefits of buying from a national retailer whose volume of business was large meant that good value could be obtained at a local branch. Burton's on the right is offering a suit for 45s, which was good value for the office worker although many employees did not earn that in a week. Slogans (such as 'Burton's: the Tailor of Taste') and large newspaper adverts were being devised by copywriters to keep the business coming in. The majority of Ilfordians still used public transport to a large degree and any rise in fares or deterioration in service would cause comment in the local newspapers. Some office workers saved money by going into London on the earliest trains to take advantage of the concessionary 'workmen's fare', one of the few cheaper tickets available. They would then kill time until their office opened. In the 1930s, the monopolised London Transport Passenger Board was created and this led to advances in bus standardisation (two LPTB six-wheeler LT-class buses can be seen) and passenger comfort. Green Line Coaches ran along the High Road – these were new express buses that stopped at selected points along the route only. These vehicles had comfortable seats and were meant to compete with the railway. Their destination was Aldgate Terminus in London, opposite the Underground station and nearer to some City offices than the overcrowded and smoky Liverpool Street.

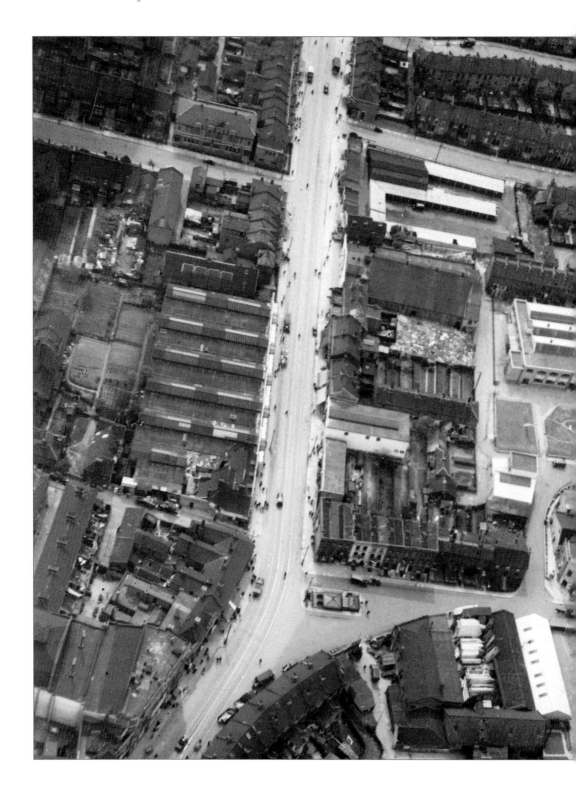

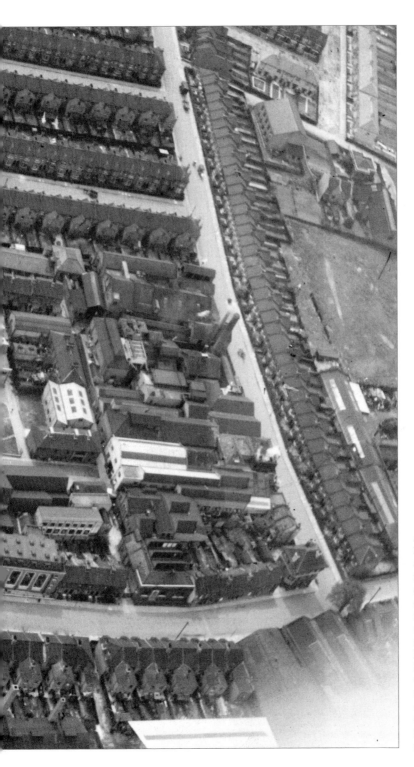

A surprising aerial view of Ilford Lane, Roden Street and the Ilford photographic film works, 1930. At left centre, where Roden Street enters Ilford Lane, were the underground public conveniences which were always very clean and well looked after. Today they lie under the middle of the widened road and the one-way traffic system devised at the end of the century. No plane today would be allowed to fly low enough to take such a shot.

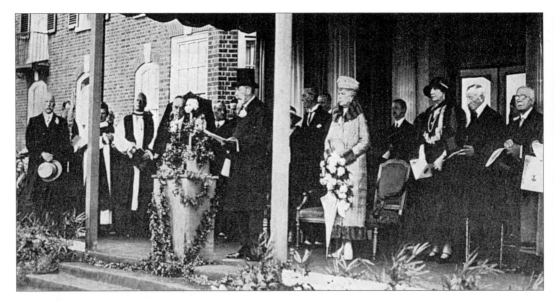

King George V and his consort Queen Mary opening the hospital named after the king, 18 July 1931. The new hospital incorporated some of the buildings of the old Ilford Emergency Hospital, but it was a large, modern facility.

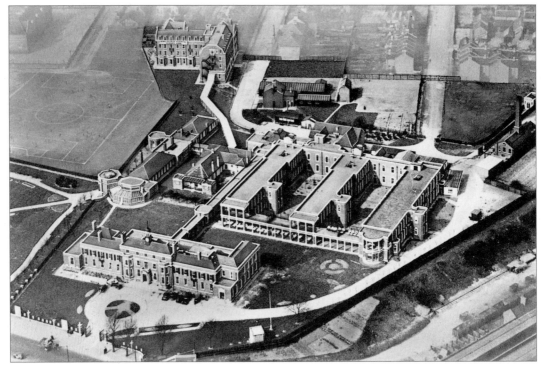

The layout of the new hospital. Eastern Avenue is at bottom left and the LNER loop line (later the Central Line) is at bottom right. Figures quoted in the 1930s claimed the hospital treated 4,500 in-patients and some 120,000 out-patients a year.

BOROUGH OF
ILFORD

ELECTRICITY
DEPARTMENT

Washing by Electricity

HOTPOINT
Electric
Washing
Machine

£25

CASH

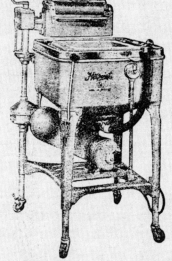

AS SELECTED
BY
HIS MAJESTY
THE KING
FOR THE
SILVER
JUBILEE
HOUSE

WILL WASH FOR A FAMILY OF
FOUR PERSONS IN ONE HOUR

A FREE DEMONSTRATION IN YOUR HOME
WILL BE GIVEN ON APPLICATION

MACHINES SUPPLIED ON EASY TERMS

Call to inspect this Washer at

THE CENTRAL ELECTRICITY SHOWROOMS
320-326, HIGH ROAD ● ILFORD

A washing machine, 1935-style, as advertised by the borough's electricity department.

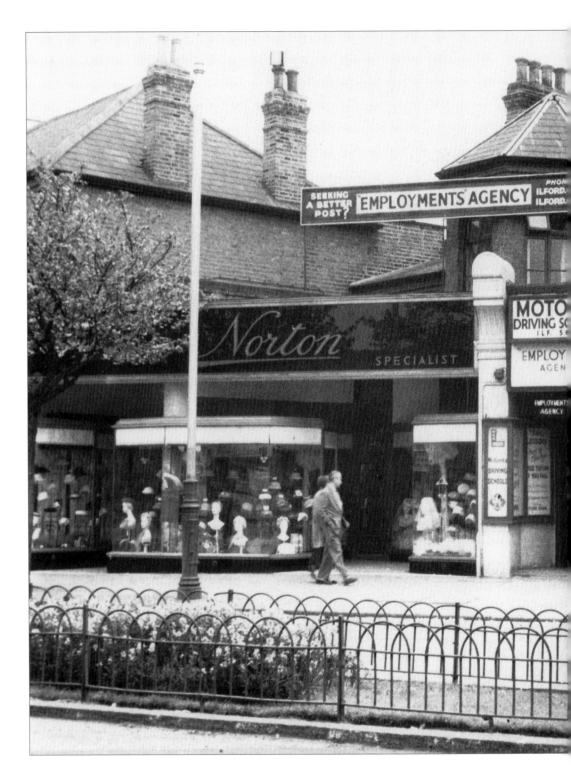

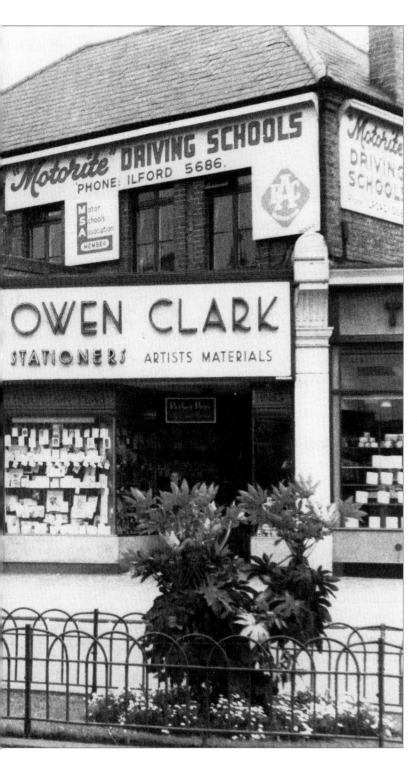

Owen Clark's, at the bend in Cranbrook Road. The varied and interesting stock of artists' materials and stationery was first displayed here in 1928. The milliners on the left, now part of Clark's, was a delightful hat shop of a kind rarely seen today – some of the hats are displayed at different levels on pole-like shop fittings. This arrangement was still to be seen in the 1970s. The name on the shop at this time was Jessie Norton but in 1931, the milliner was Peggy Fry Ltd. Notice also the Driving School and Employment Agency cheek by jowl, showing what a prosperous town Ilford had become. The municipal flowerbeds within the dwarf railings are features very typical of 1930s Britain.

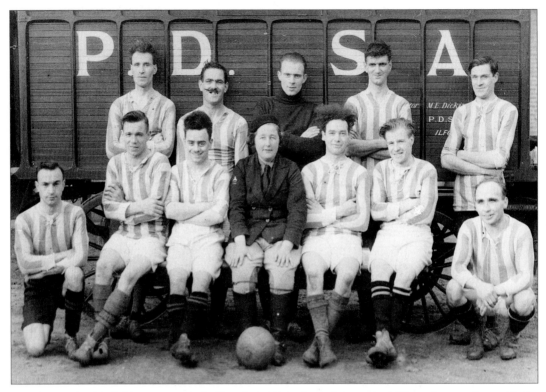

This photograph is labelled 'Sanatorium Football Match, 1933'. Back row, left to right: Williams, Dawson, Graves, Weeks, Gordon. Front row: -?-, Scott, Edwards, Adam, Carroll, Grant, Cronin. In the 1930s people generally had less leisure time so there were probably fewer organised league matches than today, but amateur matches against neighbouring businesses provided great entertainment, tremendous fun being had by all, win or lose.

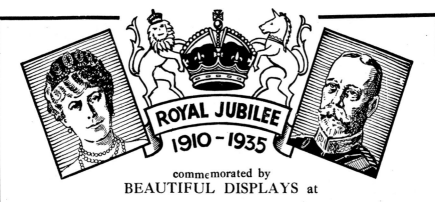

ROYAL JUBILEE
1910 - 1935

commemorated by
BEAUTIFUL DISPLAYS at

HEYWOODS

**THE NEWEST
AND BEST
IN LADIES'
COATS,
FROCKS,
KNITWEAR,
MILLINERY
UNDERWEAR, etc.**

Also

**CHILDREN'S
WEAR**

and

PIECE GOODS !

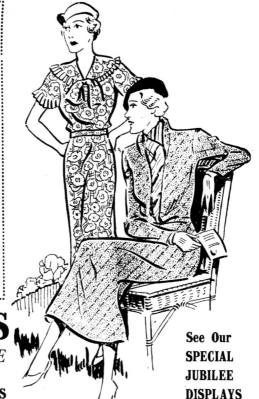

HEYWOODS

DRAPERY STORE

**645-649,
HIGH ROAD, SEVEN KINGS**

Telephone: SEVEN KINGS 1792

See Our
SPECIAL
JUBILEE
DISPLAYS

Some of the ladies' fashions of the mid-1930s on show at Heywood's as the shop celebrates the silver jubilee in 1935. Heywood's was just one of the well-known shops at Seven Kings to which people would travel from a distance. Shopping in the 1930s was still not yet completely dominated by the multiples. There was still a place for individuality and personal service.

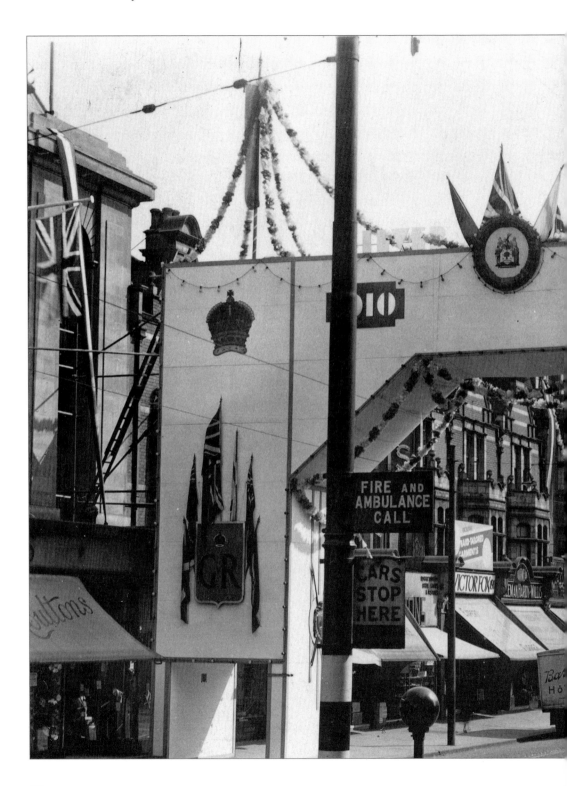

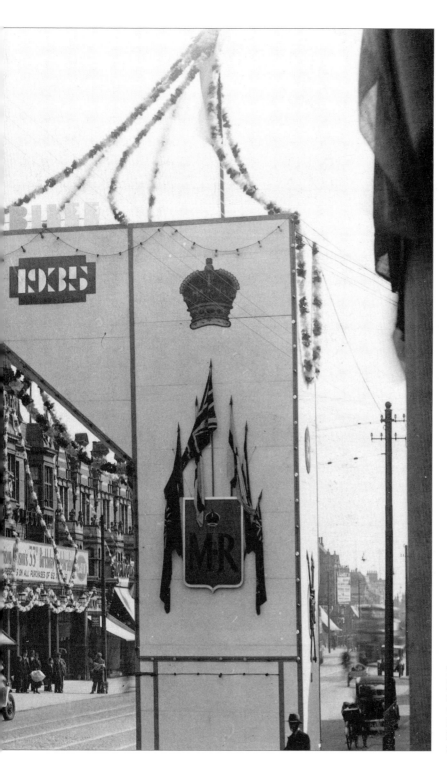

To celebrate the silver
jubilee of George V a
modernistic archway
was erected over the
High Road next to
Moultons Store (on
the left).

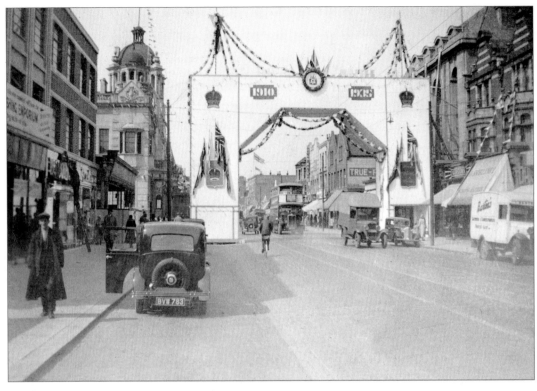

The archway in the High Road, viewed from the opposite direction. It can be clearly seen how the arch restricts the width of the road. Was this an early attempt to reduce vehicle speeds as well as celebrating the jubilee?

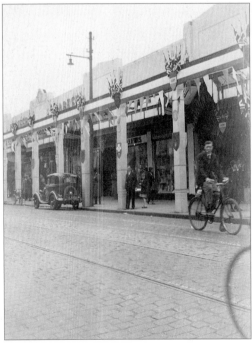

The Pioneer Market, Ilford Lane, decorated for a royal occasion, perhaps the jubilee.

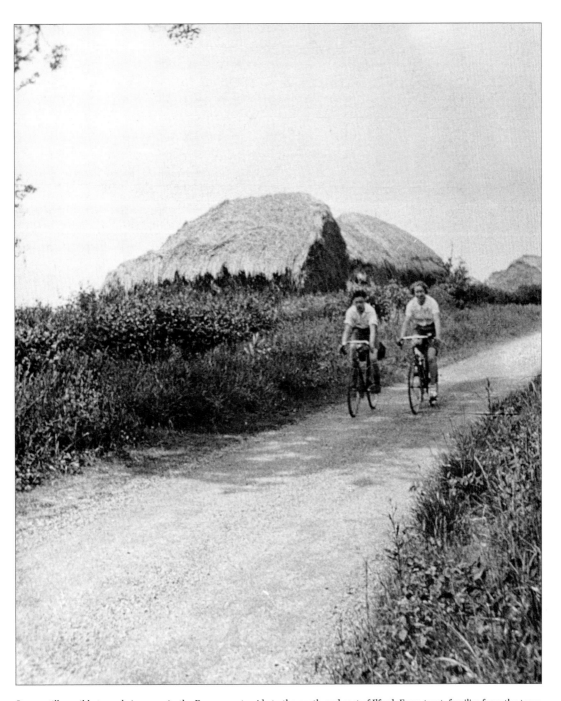

It was still possible to cycle in peace in the Essex countryside to the north and east of Ilford. For a treat, families from the town centre might take a train on the Ilford loop, get out at Fairlop or Buckhurst Hill, and then walk miles along the roads, perhaps pushing a pram with the latest arrival. They would stop at a pub or by the roadside somewhere and consume the picnic they had brought. Food was not generally available at such hostelries and anyway the pennies had to be saved!

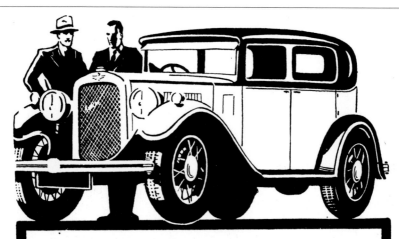

The complete service station for motorists

●

MORRIS, AUSTIN AND WOLSELEY AGENTS

●

Ask any customer of ours and you'll be told that you get valuable extra service from Smith Motors, whether you're buying a new or secondhand car. There isn't a place in the Home Counties with a wider range of cars than we keep. You come to our convenient showrooms and you have choice of a magnificent selection under most comfortable conditions. And when you've bought, we "service" you in every conceivable way, from a timely hint to a complete overhaul. We've an acre of up-to-date workshops here with brake-testing plant, high pressure lubrication and all those other modern aids to motoring. It really pays you to become one of our customers.

HEAD OFFICE, SHOWROOMS & WORKS:
HIGH ROAD, GOODMAYES, ILFORD

ILFORD DEPOT: 22, Cranbrook Road, Ilford.
ROMFORD DEPOT: South Street, Romford.
WANSTEAD DEPOT: High Street, Wanstead.

SMITH·MOTORS
GOODMAYES...ILFORD...LONDON

Phone: Seven Kings 1000 (7 lines) day and night.

More and more families were able to buy a car in the 1930s and car showrooms were springing up all around Ilford, particularly in the Goodmayes and Seven Kings areas. The days of peaceful meandering on foot along country lanes were already numbered.

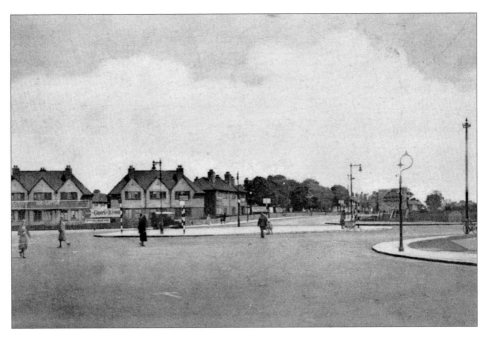

Gants Hill intersection with Eastern Avenue in its early days, before motor traffic really took off.

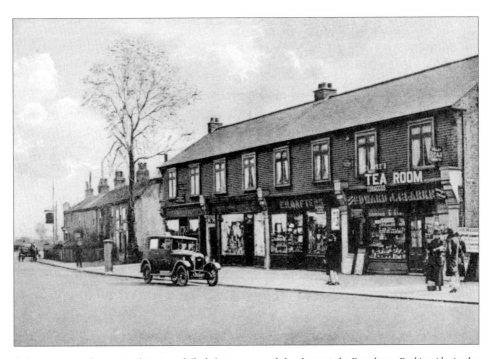

Only one car can be seen in this view of Clarke's tearoom and the shops at the Broadway, Barkingside, in the 1930s.

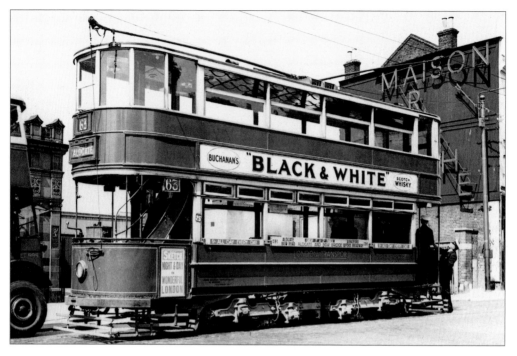

Tram no. 310 on route 63 bound for Aldgate waits by the Red Lion, Ilford Broadway, 7 June 1938.

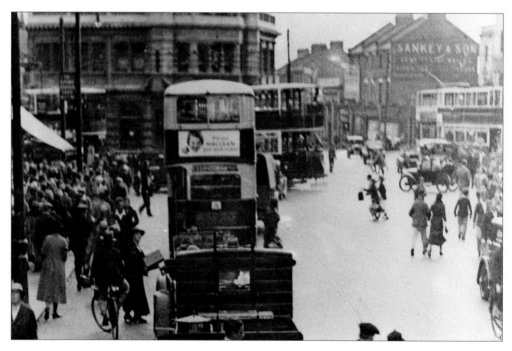

A very busy day at Ilford Broadway in the mid-1930s. Pedestrians, cars, buses and trams compete for space.

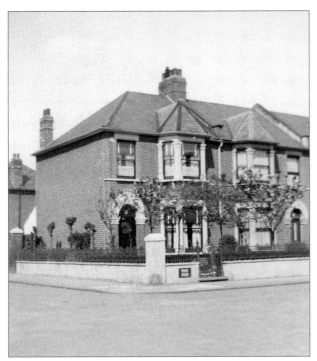

In the side roads around Ilford it could still be very quiet. This is No. 58 Park Road in May 1937.

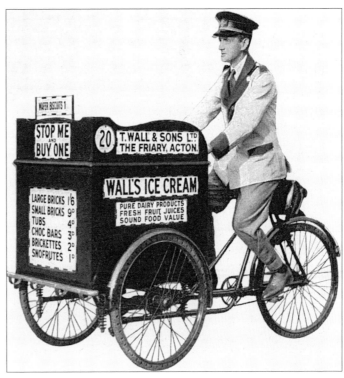

The ice-cream tricycle was a familiar sight on the roads at this time.

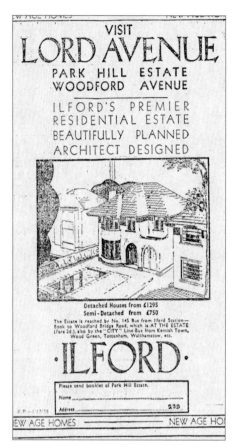

Superior houses for sale on the Park Hill Estate, December 1936.

The new Ilford telephone exchange (code: VALentine) was built over what was once the Wash, a watersplash pond into which cart drivers drove their horses to cool off on hot days.

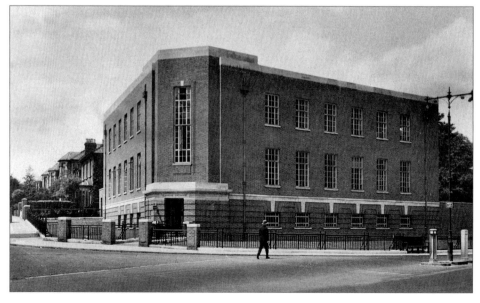

Conflict and Austerity

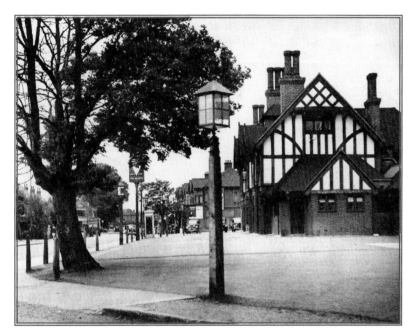

Beehive Lane and the Beehive public house in the late 1930s. The Beehive was an ultra-stylish building, but the fine Art Deco lamps were soon to be doused, in accordance with the new blackout regulations instituted as the Second World War began. The blackout was an extra problem for local residents and took some getting used to – unlit streets, public transport with severely reduced lights, traffic lights cut down to coloured crosses. In the winter months Ilfordians went to work in the dark and returned home in the dark, having to deal every night with the blackout curtains, hoping no warden would shout 'put that light out'. Where the curtains were inadequate there was experimentation with all kinds of ingenious substitutes. Public areas such as kerbs, lamp-posts and station platform edges were painted white in an effort reduce the number of serious accidents.

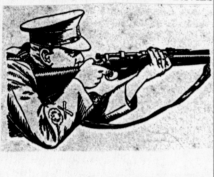

THE HOME GUARD TRAINING MANUAL

Based by permission on War Office Instruction Books

By MAJOR JOHN LANGDON-DAVIES

JOHN MURRAY & THE PILOT PRESS

Required reading for those who joined the Home Guard. The training manual and similar publications were very serious in their intention. In spite of the humour directed at the Home Guard's activities and the high average age of its members, there was a wealth of experience within its ranks to deal with the anticipated emergencies.

Anti-aircraft advice was probably largely a morale booster for the average Home Guard recruit. Initially the Home Guard was known as the Local Defence Volunteers (LDV), and two months after formation the king came to inspect the local battalions on parade at Woodford RUFC ground. Selected men were sent to operate the properly equipped anti-aircraft sites such as that in Whalebone Lane, which was able to mount a strong defence against enemy planes.

160   ANTI-AIRCRAFT

(b) If a low-flying bomber which you have been observing lets fly a bomb you will almost certainly have plenty of time to fall on your face. Always try to lie lower than the ground level. If you are being machine-gunned you will be safest standing up.

(c) If a dive-bomber attacks you, the chances of its scoring a direct hit are very small indeed and you will be far safer staying where you are than if you run. Always try to have enough cover to protect you from fragments and from blast. Remember that the enemy's object is probably to force you to give ground and that by sticking it out you defeat the enemy's plans.

(d) It is not enough to stop where you are and do nothing if there is any chance of your being able to hit back at the bomber. This can be done with a great chance of success if the proper rules about firing are kept.

3. It is useless to try and hit a plane flying at more than two thousand feet.

It is useless for individuals to shoot off their rifles on their own. All firing must be done by small groups firing together under the control of a leader.

Sights must be set at five hundred yards.

The time that the plane will be in range is very small indeed and every care must be taken that there is no firing before or after this brief period.

4. The following are the words of command that will be given by the group commander;

(a) **Aircraft Action.** Adopt standing load position with rifle as vertical as possible, and load, leaving safety-catch forward.

(b) **Aircraft Front** (Right, Left, About). Turn in direction ordered, keeping rifle up. Bring rifle to aiming position, finger on trigger; take first pressure, aim and begin to swing.

(c) **Rapid Fire.** Open fire until "stop" is given.

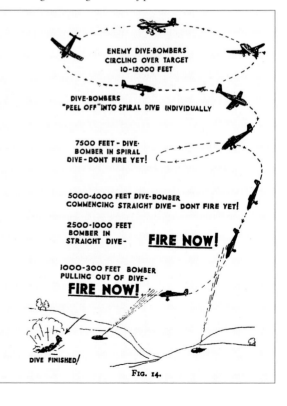

ENEMY DIVE-BOMBERS
CIRCLING OVER TARGET
10-12000 FEET

DIVE-BOMBERS
"PEEL OFF"INTO SPIRAL DIVE INDIVIDUALLY

7500 FEET - DIVE-
BOMBER IN SPIRAL
DIVE-DONT FIRE YET!

5000-4000 FEET DIVE-BOMBER
COMMENCING STRAIGHT DIVE- DONT FIRE YET!

2500-1000 FEET
BOMBER IN
STRAIGHT DIVE- **FIRE NOW!**

1000-300 FEET BOMBER
PULLING OUT OF DIVE-
FIRE NOW!

DIVE FINISHED!

FIG. 14.

AIR DEFENCE AND PRECAUTION

(See also Domestic Services (Veterinary), Emergency Services, Health (Hospital), Territorial Army and Youth Organisations.)

AIR RAID PRECAUTIONS.—Borough of Ilford:

Responsible Authority: Ilford Borough Council.
Committee: Civil Defence (Emergency).
Enquiries: All enquiries relative to Air Raid Precautions should be made to the Town Clerk, Town Hall, Ilford.

PUBLIC AIR RAID SHELTERS:

Shelters for the use of the public are provided in the majority of *Parks* in the Borough and many empty shop properties and other suitable premises have been taken over and converted into shelters. The *positions of all shelters are adequately indicated on the public highway* and any Burgesses in doubt as to the nearest public shelter for their use when caught in the street should consult the nearest Air Raid Wardens.
(As many public shelters are being provided from time to time it is not considered advisable that the positions of shelters should be referred to for use in conjunction with the Street Plan.)

AIR RAID WARDENS' POSTS, AUXILIARY FIRE STATIONS, ETC.:

Any Air Raid Warden will be in a position to advise any person in doubt as to the nearest Air Raid Warden's Post and Auxiliary Fire Station to his residence. Altogether 88 *Wardens' Posts* have been established in the Borough, together with an *adequate number of Auxiliary Fire Stations and Auxiliary Fire Service Action Stations* to serve the area.

Air Raid Precautions information from the *Borough of Ilford Record, Year Book and Street Plan*, 1940, one of the few local directories to continue into the war. Ilford Borough at the time was small enough for local people to identify with and therefore to know what they were fighting for.

Hand-grenade training notes from the *Home Guard Manual*. If the German invasion had taken place, a 'secret army' of highly trained men would have been engaged in harrying the enemy constantly by use of such weapons and guerrilla tactics. They would have operated from a secret bunker in woodland to the far east of Ilford. It was Winston Churchill's idea to create a British Resistance Organisation in 1940. Under cover of the Home Guard, in which many had enlisted before being asked to join these so-called Auxiliary Units, secrecy was maintained.

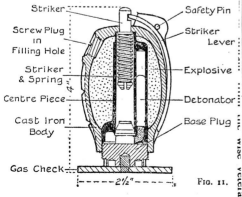

HAND GRENADES   131

man will pick up a grenade which has been thrown, until ordered to do so.

These instructions must be rigidly obeyed, in order that, from the very start, you will instinctively learn to treat grenades with respect. There is no need to be nervous with a grenade, however, as long as you understand it.

4. Throwing practice with live grenades will only take place on a grenade range and under a qualified instructor as defined in Home Guard Training Instruction.

5. The following diagrams will make the nature of hand grenade practice perfectly clear to you.

FIG. 11.

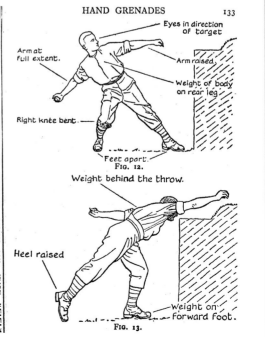

HAND GRENADES   133

FIG. 12.

Weight behind the throw.

FIG. 13.

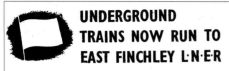

UNDERGROUND TRAINS NOW RUN TO EAST FINCHLEY L·N·E·R

Highgate Station L·N·E·R will open for Underground Services Summer, 1940.

1939

AUTUMN. BAKERLOO LINE. Baker Street to Finchley Road : through trains between Elephant & Castle and Stanmore.

1940

SPRING. NORTHERN LINE. East Finchley to High Barnet : through trains between High Barnet and Morden.

SPRING. CENTRAL LINE. North Acton to Greenford : through trains between Greenford and Liverpool Street.

SPRING. CENTRAL LINE. Liverpool Street to Loughton and Hainault (via Woodford) : through trains between Greenford, Loughton and Hainault.

SUMMER. CENTRAL LINE. Greenford to Ruislip : through trains between Ruislip and Loughton.

AUTUMN. NORTHERN LINE. Drayton Park to Alexandra Palace : through trains between Alexandra Palace and High Barnet and Moorgate.

1941

SPRING. CENTRAL LINE. Loughton to Ongar : and Leytonstone to Woodford via Newbury Park : through trains, Loughton, Hainault and Ruislip (via Woodford), Hainault and Ruislip (via Newbury Park).

SPRING. NORTHERN LINE. Finchley (Church End) to Bushey Heath : through trains between Bushey Heath and Morden.

SPRING. METROPOLITAN LINE. Harrow to Rickmansworth, widening : Rickmansworth to Amersham and Chesham electrification.

London Transport: *Future Expectations*, 1939–41. The outbreak of war prevented the opening of the planned extension of the Central Line to Loughton, Hainault and Ongar over the old LNER above-ground line with new tunnels in North Ilford, as described in the leaflet.

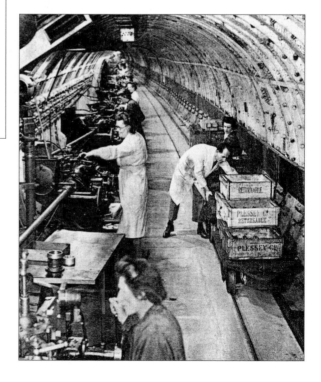

Instead of becoming part of Ilford's transport facilities the nearly finished tunnels between Leytonstone and Newbury Park were taken over by Plessey Co. and pressed into service as aircraft component factories, which opened in 1942. Note on the right the narrow-gauge rails used to transport materials. The factory was 5 miles long and employed 2,000 workers, and the air-conditioning system was a triumph of engineering.

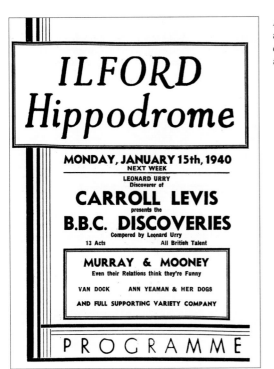

A wartime programme for the Hippodrome. *Discoveries* was an earlier version of today's *Stars in their Eyes*. After initially closing all theatres in 1939 the government reopened them again in the interests of maintaining morale.

What happened next? The Hippodrome certainly did its bit to cheer people up in dangerous times, running more or less nightly entertainment throughout the war years, including pantomimes for the children (*Red Riding Hood*, for instance, at Christmas 1939/New Year 1940). Unfortunately, on 21 January 1945 the building was hit by a rocket and the explosion devastated the theatre and nearby cottages. This was the scene inside the auditorium. The shell of the building remained standing for many years until debris started to fall into the street, endangering public safety. It was subsequently demolished.

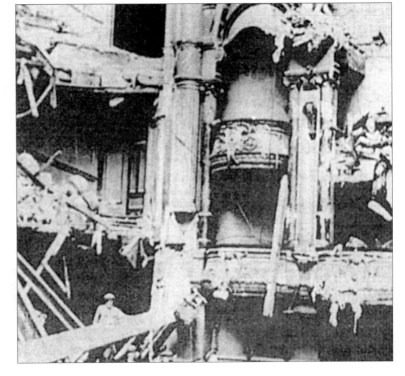

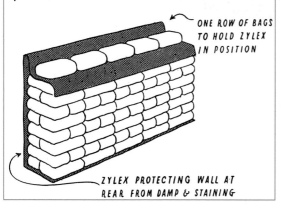
Many buildings in Ilford were surrounded by sandbag walls to protect them from the blast of explosions. Vera Perrott spoke of passing through the gloomy sandbagged corridors of the Girls' High School. The bags were subject to deterioration, however, if not reinforced.

Local firms adapted their production and services to wartime needs.

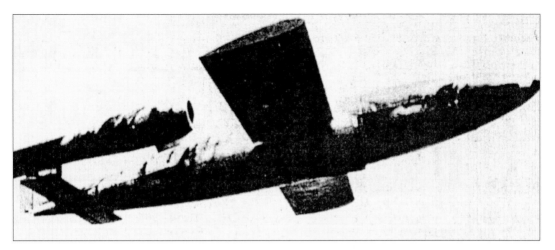

A V1 'Doodlebug' or pilotless rocket glides through the air on its way to England. It was common for residents to watch them pass overhead, the engine pulsing like a motorbike's and with a red glow at the rear. Suddenly the engine would stop and everyone would dive for cover; in the eerie silence that followed, you prayed that it had not stopped directly overhead. The silence would be followed by the muffled roar of the explosion after the weapon had landed. Fifty-nine of these flying bombs fell in the vicinity of Ilford.

Incident No.	Time	Location of Incident.	Area of Launching	Other Information
257	0540	VL904405 Between CAPEL GARDENS and LONGBRIDGE ROAD, ILFORD. (Corrected pin-point).	MONSTER Area.	Additional Information:- 5 houses demolished and 20 seriously damaged. 4 persons killed 6 seriously injured 3 trapped Radar Ranges:- Dunkirk 142.4 to 121.9 miles Time 0534 06/60 to 0534 48/60 hrs Bromley 130.3 to 126.6 miles Time 0534 00/60 to 0534 22/60 hrs Bawdsey 115.1 to 93.2 miles Time 0534 03/60 to 0534 49/60 hrs High Street 112.5 to 96.2 miles Time 0534 to 0534 44/60 hrs Based on range cuts, the Scientific Observer estimates the firing point to be within an area 2 Kms East of a line QD 5880 to QD 5884.

The incident report of an even more terrifying weapon, the V2 rocket. This strike, one of forty-nine in the area, pulverised the houses between Capel Gardens and Longbridge Road in November 1944. This new weapon came suddenly and unannounced to terrorise Britain in the last months of the war, when we already had a foothold in Europe. The government was unwilling to acknowledge the nature of this new terror at first, giving out information that such incidents were the result of gas explosions. The rockets sped out of the sky at 3,000 mph. The security services gave them the codename 'Big Ben'. Strangely, survivors of 'near-misses' often reported hearing very little noise.

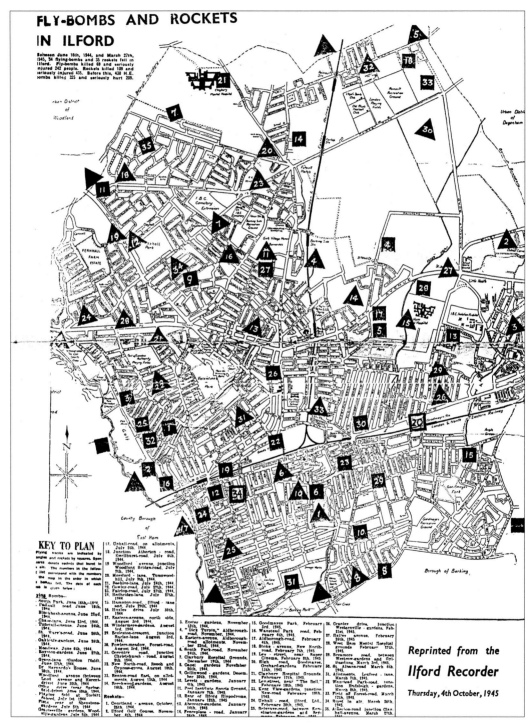

There was a V1 or V2 incident in nearly every part of Ilford in 1944/5.

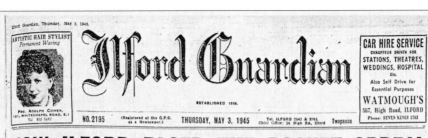

Ilford Guardian

ESTABLISHED 1899.

NO. 2195   (Registered at the G.P.O. as a Newspaper)   THURSDAY, MAY 3, 1945   Tel. ILFORD 3143 & 2763, Chief Office: 34 High Rd., Ilford   Twopence

HOW ILFORD FACED THE ROCKET ORDEAL

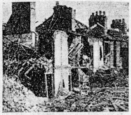

Wreckage is piled high around the war-scarred skeleton of a house in Ley Street.

ONE OF THE WORST HIT BOROUGHS
STORIES OF HEROISM AND MIRACULOUS ESCAPES
FIVE MONTHS OF TENSION

The story can now be told of how Ilford, one of London's most heavily hit rocket districts, faced the terror offensive by the V1 and faced it with a grim determination and heroism that will long be remembered in the history of the Borough. Never knowing when the blow would fall the people carried on with their normal routine. The high morale and bravery of the residents was especially commendable as the offensive by the new weapon followed closely on the flying bomb attacks and meant further long nights of flying bomb attacks and meant further long nights of the V2 could be heard for miles away.

Some areas which had already been damaged by the flying bombs had to face a further ordeal of death and destruction by a weapon, which unlike the flying bomb, gave no warning. Green Lane, Ley Street and Wanstead Park Road are places which suffered severely from both forms of attack. Many tales can be told of the bravery of the injured, of the magnificent work of the rescue and repair squads who worked day and night, of miraculous escapes and tragic deaths.

When the last V2 crashed in Ilford just over three weeks ago it ended an ordeal of a Borough which has been hard hit by every kind of air bombardment devised by the Germans since 1940. Ilford will long show its scars of battle but is slowly getting its house in order again.

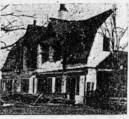

"The Dick Turpin," a well known landmark in Aldborough Hatch, which was severely damaged in one of the first V-bomb incidents in Ilford.

"ON THE JOB" WITHIN TEN MINUTES
REPAIR SQUADS WORKED THROUGH THE NIGHT

"THE EYES AND EARS OF THE C.D"
HOW ILFORD'S 2,000 WARDENS PULLED THEIR WEIGHT

WHEN THE SUPER WAS DAMAGED

ILFORD M.P.
ASKS ABOUT ROCKET ATTACKS ... IN THE HOUSE.

ALMOST ASLEEP STANDING UP
RESCUE SERVICES' GRUELLING ORDEAL

MAYOR IS "MORE THAN PROUD"
OF ILFORDIANS' COURAGE

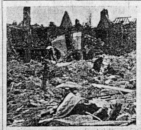

Bombed out women search among the rubble that was once their homes for their possessions. A pathetic scene at the St. Alban's Rd. incident, in which 1,108 houses were affected.

There was initially a sense of shock at the ferocity of the onslaught but soon newspapers were full of praise for the efficiency and heroism of local civil defence workers and civilians. Other reports told of miraculous escapes.

HONOUR   FREEDOM

MEMBERS OF   THE STAFF OF

GOODMAYES

L.M.F.S.

SERVING IN H.M. FORCES AND CIVIL DEFENCE.

M.H.Bacon.	K.R.R.	A.J.Mills.	R.A.F.
R.A.Boddington.	R.A.F.	E.Mudd.	P.W.R.
C.W.Crabb.	R.A.F.	J.O'Shea.	A.M.P.C.
A.E.Cross.	R.A.F.	J.S.Parker.	N.J.S.
B.H.Deleeuw.	R.A.F.	W.Perkins.	R.N.
J.Dell.	P.W.R.	G.J.Pickford.	R.A.
E.J.Dinmore.	4.M.R.	A.W.Richards.	N.J.S.
J.Foster.	W.R.	S.A.Rickwood.	R.A.F.
A.W.Freeman.	R.A.	J.A.Salmon.	R.A.F.
A.Grey.	P.W.R.	J.C.Spencer.	R.N.
J.J.Hilton.	R.A.S.C.	G.A.Thornton.	R.E.
R.Knight.	R.A.F.	H.Townsend.	R.A.S.C
A.E.Kay.	R.A.S.C.	E.Woolger.	D.W.R.
E.Mack.	M.G.C.		

This card showing Goodmayes' Locally Maintained Fire Service was the contribution of one organisation to the armed forces and emergency services during the war.

Once the war was over the battle was on to organise the orderly release of the huge numbers of servicemen and women. New words were bandied about, such as 'demobbed', 'civvy' and 'erk'. For some Ilfordians it took years to settle down again on Civvy Street after their change of role.

ILFORD MAN ONE OF THE FIRST DEMOBBED

AFTER OVER FOUR YEARS IN R.A.F.

On Monday A/C1 Charles Cutler, of 49 Valentines Road, Ilford, ceased to be an "erk" and became a "civvie" once again. He is probably the first Ilford man to return home under the demobilisation scheme, and in his own words, "feels wonderfully free to be home again and walking about in a civvy suit."

On Sunday night, A/C1 Cutler slept in a hut with a number of other members of the R.A.F. who were placed together irrespective of rank. On Monday morning their first job was to hand in most of their kit, although they retained their uniforms. "Alongside me were two Warrant Officers, lugging their blankets along with them—the same as we were—there was strict equality," he said. "I was very impressed, both at the courtesy and the organisation of those who were supervising the demobilisation.

"The Commanding Officer was walking round asking us if everything was running smoothly and satisfactorily. I replied laughingly 'Yes, only you don't get treated the same as this when you come in!'

A quarter of an hour sufficed for the distribution of his demobilisation papers, pay, and papers enabling him to obtain his identity card and ration book. After this he was fitted out with a complete set of civilian clothes.

"The whole affair was arranged with something like the organisa-tion of an exhibition," he said. "You went in one end, were ushered here and there, and went out the other end completely fitted out. I tried on thirty coats before I decided on one which suited me.

"We were given far more consideration than we would have received in a west-end store, and after we had picked a suit if eventually we decided that we didn't like it, we could always change it.

"I tried on five pairs of shoes before I picked the pair I wanted. We were completely fitted out, even down to a pair of cuff-links.

"A coach took us down to the station, where a type of N.A.A.F.I. made us quite happy, and I was home by just before three in the afternoon."

A/C Cutler has been in the Air Force for 4½ years as a fitter general. At home to greet him were his sister and three nephews, all of whom are in the services. He is eager to get back into his pre-war trade as an engineer. He is unmarried.

One legacy of the war was this SA Class trolley-bus no. 1752 (in front). These vehicles had been built for South Africa but when the war began they were diverted for use here to replace war-damaged vehicles.

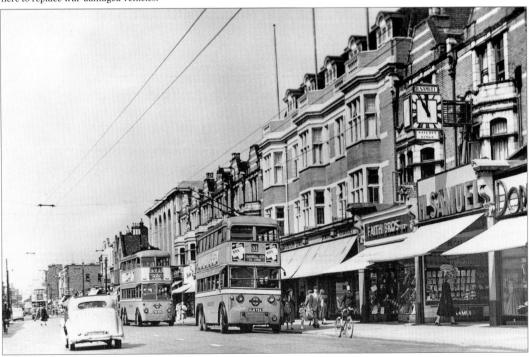

THE FUEL CRISIS
AND YOU

How can you save that VITAL QUARTER of your GAS and ELECTRICITY?

THE FIRST STEPS ARE

1 *Get to know your meters and read them regularly.*
2 *Find out your consumption last summer and so arrive at your target figure.*
3 *Know how much fuel each gas or electrical appliance uses.*

SLOT METERS. Most slot meters can be read in the same way as ordinary meters—but if you are in difficulty then the simplest rule is to use not more than 3/- where you are in the habit of using 4/-, or 3d. instead of 4d.

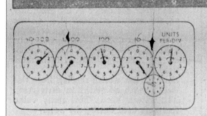

HOW TO READ YOUR ELECTRICITY METER

Ignore the small test dial below. Write down the reading of the dials from left to right.

When the hand is between two figures put down the smaller one (but if between 9 and 0 put down 9).

When the hand is on a figure put down one less, except when the hand on the next dial to the right has just passed 0. (The meter above reads 13960 not 14960).

Read your meter at the same time on the same day each week.

Subtract last week's reading from this week's. The answer shows how many electricity units were used during the week.

ELECTRICAL APPLIANCES AND THEIR CONSUMPTION

Most appliances are marked with their wattage. Equipment marked 250W uses ¼ unit per hour; that marked 1000W or 1 KW uses 1 unit per hour; 2 KW, 2 units per hour and so on.

Figures given cannot be exactly correct for every appliance. They simply show how long average appliances operate for one unit.

Appliance	Time of operation	Appliance	Time of operation
Immersion Heater	20 minutes	Kettle	1 hour
Wash Boiler	20 minutes	Toaster	2 hours
Sink Storage Heater	30 minutes	Electric Iron	2 to 3 hours
Oven (on full)	40 minutes	Vacuum Cleaner	6 hours
Grill (on full)	½ to 1 hour	60 watt lamp	16 hours
Boiling Plate (on full)	½ to 1 hour	Radio	20 hours
Fire (one bar)	½ to 1 hour	Refrigerator	1 day

Very soon Ilfordians had to cope with an official fuel crisis caused by cold winters and the shortage of resources following a very expensive war that had depleted the nation's treasury.

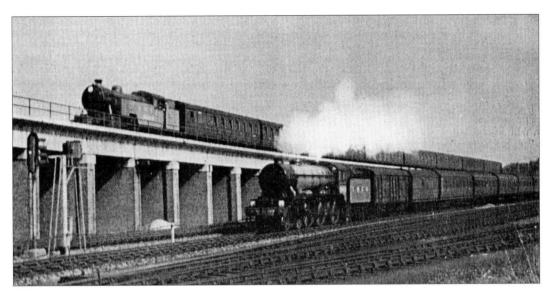

In connection with the Liverpool Street–Shenfield electrification scheme, the Ilford flyover was opened for train traffic on 6 October 1947.

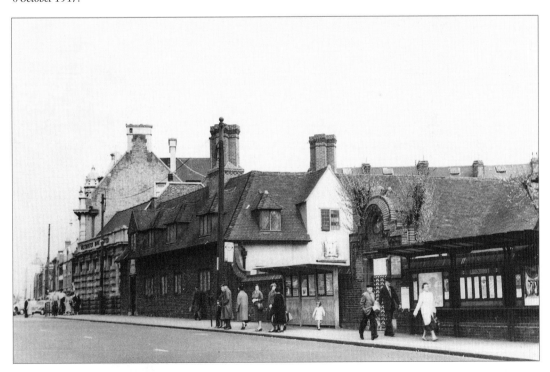

Waiting for buses on Ilford Hill. It took a long time for the bus industry to recover from wartime conditions and to begin developing and building new vehicles. But when the machines finally arrived they were some of the best anywhere; indeed, many people still believe the Routemaster bus has never been bettered. Meanwhile, passengers put up with problems by calling on the patience they had developed in wartime.

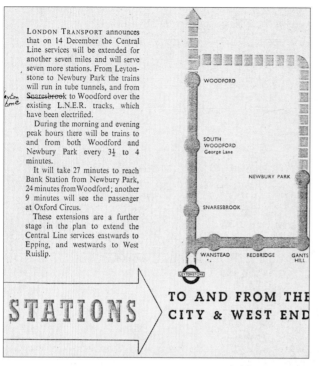

LONDON TRANSPORT announces that on 14 December the Central Line services will be extended for another seven miles and will serve seven more stations. From Leytonstone to Newbury Park the trains will run in tube tunnels, and from Snaresbrook to Woodford over the existing L.N.E.R. tracks, which have been electrified.

During the morning and evening peak hours there will be trains to and from both Woodford and Newbury Park every 3½ to 4 minutes.

It will take 27 minutes to reach Bank Station from Newbury Park, 24 minutes from Woodford; another 9 minutes will see the passenger at Oxford Circus.

These extensions are a further stage in the plan to extend the Central Line services eastwards to Epping, and westwards to West Ruislip.

STATIONS > TO AND FROM THE CITY & WEST END

One railway development was given priority — the opening of the new Central Line link north-eastwards from Leytonstone over the LNER route. This used the tunnel that had been turned into a wartime Plessey factory. It really put North Ilford on the map, with Bank station in the City now only 27 minutes from Newbury Park. The text of this official leaflet has been corrected by an official in handwriting. These stations were opened in November 1947.

The newly completed Gants Hill concourse.

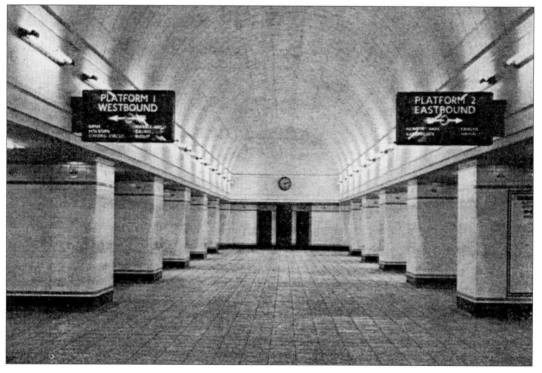

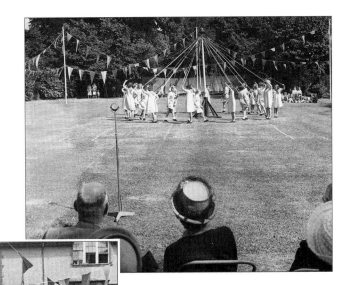

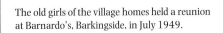

The old girls of the village homes held a reunion at Barnardo's, Barkingside, in July 1949.

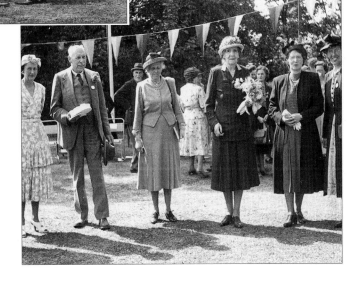

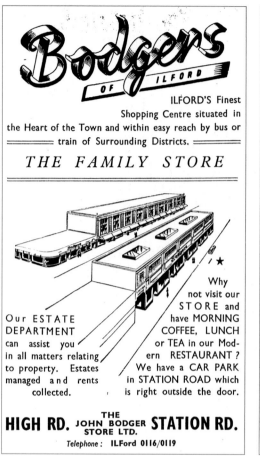
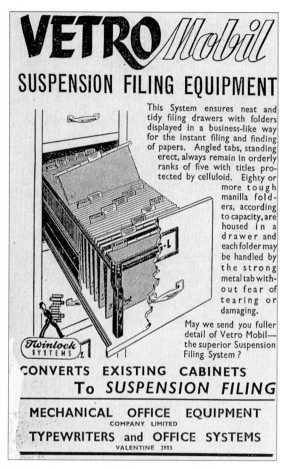
The postwar British economy gradually began to pick up and by 1952 both the retail sector in the town (represented here by Bodgers) and manufacturers (the Mechanical Office Equipment Co.) flexed their muscles and advertised their wares.

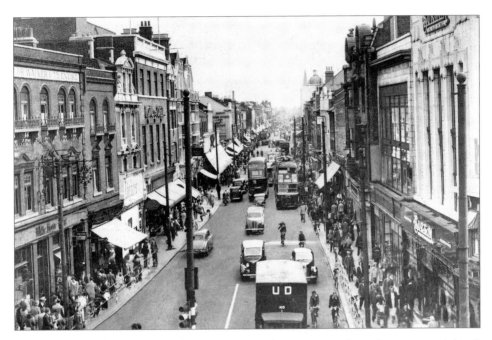

As petrol became more readily available larger numbers of cars appeared on the roads. Yet many people still walked to the shops and most children walked to school. The pavements along the High Road are crowded in this scene and safety railings have been installed from the Broadway corner.

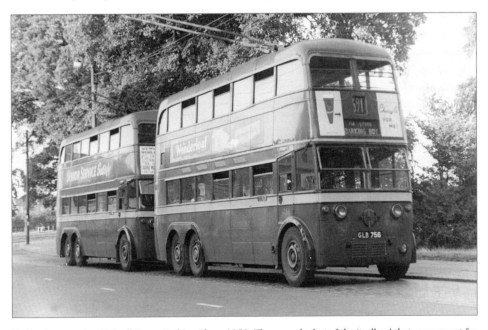

Trolley-buses wait at Fulwell Cross, Barkingside, c. 1959. These are the last of the 'trolleys' that were meant for South Africa, and they had tinted glass designed to reduce the glare of the African sun. Great demands were still being made on public transport and petrol-engined buses were soon to replace the trolleys on all routes.

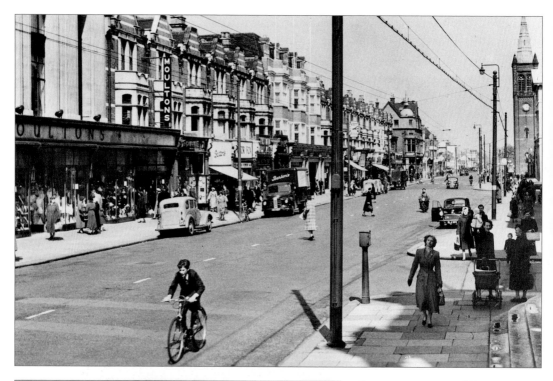

The postwar pavements of Ilford High Road with Moultons original store on the left.

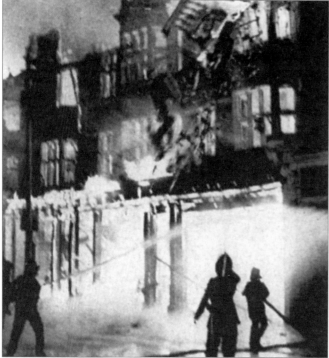

Fire broke out at Harrison Gibson's on 16 March 1959 and quickly spread to Moultons, burning out both shops. About 200 firemen attended the blaze with 40 fire appliances, one of which is reported to have come from as far away as Harwich.

Modern Ilford:
Style and Structure

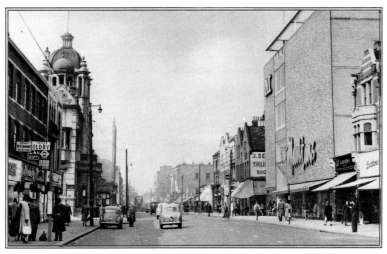

The rebuilt Moultons store ushers in an era of larger buildings. The fire pictured opposite marked a significant turning-point. The pace of life was accelerating. Even local authorities were to get bigger. Ilford Borough was merged into the larger London Borough of Redbridge, together with the old Wanstead and Woodford boroughs. But the old town hall on the High Road remains a centre for many municipal activities. Some quite atrocious tall buildings were erected from this time on, destroying much of the unity of the gradually evolving town that had served its citizens so well in the past. Motor vehicles of all kinds, from Minis to the giant lorries now used to deliver our home comforts, are cited as the villains of the piece, requiring huge swathes of new highways and gigantic parking areas. In compensation, the town has gained an attractive pedestrianised centre and a light and airy shopping area, the Exchange, which cleverly links High Road and the station. Traffic dodging in these parts of the town has become a thing of the past, except when an emergency services vehicle attends an incident. However, among the towers of New Ilford an older heart beats, and relics of the past – sometimes visible, sometimes hidden – linger on.

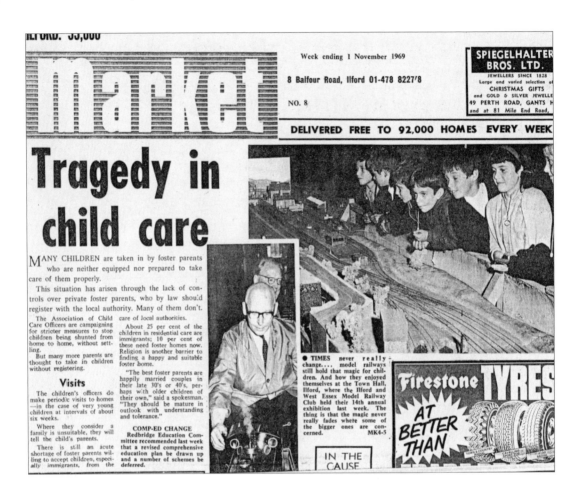

ILFORD. 55,000

Market

Week ending 1 November 1969

8 Balfour Road, Ilford 01-478 8227/8

NO. 8

SPIEGELHALTER BROS. LTD.
JEWELLERS SINCE 1828
Large and varied selection of
CHRISTMAS GIFTS
and GOLD & SILVER JEWELLE
49 PERTH ROAD, GANTS H
and at 81 Mile End Road,

DELIVERED FREE TO 92,000 HOMES EVERY WEEK

Tragedy in child care

MANY CHILDREN are taken in by foster parents who are neither equipped nor prepared to take care of them properly.

This situation has arisen through the lack of controls over private foster parents, who by law should register with the local authority. Many of them don't.

The Association of Child Care Officers are campaigning for stricter measures to stop children being shunted from home to home, without settling.

But many more parents are thought to take in children without registering.

Visits

The children's officers do make periodic visits to homes —in the case of very young children at intervals of about six weeks.

Where they consider a family is unsuitable, they will tell the child's parents.

There is still an acute shortage of foster parents willing to accept children, especially immigrants, from the care of local authorities.

About 25 per cent of the children in residential care are immigrants; 10 per cent of these need foster homes now. Religion is another barrier to finding a happy and suitable foster home.

"The best foster parents are happily married couples in their late 30's or 40's, perhaps with older children of their own," said a spokesman. "They should be mature in outlook with understanding and tolerance."

COMP-ED CHANGE

Redbridge Education Committee recommended last week that a revised comprehensive education plan be drawn up and a number of schemes be deferred.

● TIMES never really change.... model railways still hold that magic for children. And how they enjoyed themselves at the Town Hall, Ilford, where the Ilford and West Essex Model Railway Club held their 14th annual exhibition last week. The thing is that the magic never really fades where some of the bigger ones are concerned.   MK4-5

IN THE CAUSE

Firestone TYRES
AT BETTER THAN

A sign of the times. In the late 1960s one of the earliest free newspapers appeared, with a particularly populist community and consumer approach. Its name was *Market*, underlining the advertising opportunities available.

CITIZENS' ADVICE

by DOREEN McQUEEN

Your problem is theirs

THE WOMAN was clearly distressed. "It's my cat. He's gone and I was wondering if you could help me find him." The man at the desk looked across at her, understandingly. He asked for details. "Well, he ran away three years ago. . . ."

He might have collapsed in astonishment but he concealed his surprise. In his job as organising secretary of the Citizens' Advice Bureau, missing cats or the responsibility for condensation — it is all a part of the day's work.

Mr. G. J. Osborne and his staff cope with problems ranging from the seemingly minor aggravations to the important decisions concern-ing family troubles, including divorce.

They help sort out troubles concerning housing or discuss the best way to go about making a will or an accident claim. The list is long and varied but each case is dealt with understandingly and on its individual merits.

Mr. Osborne's staff of 14 are volunteers. Solicitors, accountants and a tax officer are in the team — but it isn't only professional qualifications that make the bureau

a success. The ability to communicate and the personality which must go with it are key qualities.

The bureau draws its helpers from all walks of life — those without training of any sort but with the right assets attend training courses, and "once you get your teeth into the work," says Mr. Osborne, "you become entirely immersed and can't let it go."

He has been with the bureau now for two years, and finds the work "totally absorbing."

"Each inquiry is of interest," he says. "For instance, most people don't know much about law — in their imagination a situation can seem far worse than it really is.

"They often feel nervous about coming, many feeling their particular problem is unique, but often we can put them at their ease, first by telling them it isn't, then offering concrete advice."

A problem shared — as the old saying goes. . . .

And if the C.A.B. can't give actual help required, they can put you in touch with the right people.

Intermingled with the serious side of life come the funnier instances — like the man who wanted to know how much of his favourite brand of beer he could legally take out of the country when he went on holiday, without paying duty on it!

Or the woman who wanted to do something about her husband, whom she suspected of "running around" with another woman — later in conversation she mentioned she, also, had a boyfriend.

A larger percentage of women attend the bureau,

probably because — says Mr. Osborne — of the hours, which are: weekdays 10 to 12 p.m. and 2 to 4 p.m. (there are only two evening sessions, Thursday and Friday, 6 to 8 p.m.). And unless the problem is severe, men won't take time off work during the week.

In his office at the Fellowship Hall, Green Lane, Ilford, Mr. Osborne spoke of his hopes for extending the bureau. They already hold meetings on Thursday afternoons at Wanstead Community Centre, and would like to increase these and perhaps hold sessions in the Hainault area sometime in the future. In fact, many of their inquiries come from these places.

Before he became the C.A.B. organiser at Ilford, Mr. Osborne worked as an assistant secretary for a trade charity and always had a great interest in legal problems. Now he feels he has found his forte and, as he said, like most people working for the bureau, he is totally absorbed in his work.

He is also proud of his fellow workers whom he describes as "professionals to their fingertips." Many who, though retired from full-time occupation, still use their professional knowledge and experience to the advantage of their fellow men.

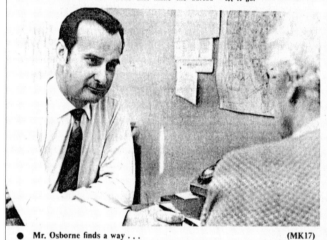

● Mr. Osborne finds a way . . .   (MK17)

Citizen's Advice Bureaux were coming into fashion in the 1960s.

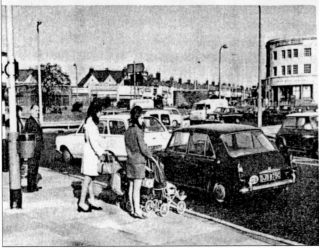

SAFETY FOR PRAM PUSHERS

—but will others still dice with death?

"IT took us a quarter of an hour to cross the road just now," said Mrs. Maureen Kiesner and Mrs. Annabella Landon, both of Gants Hill.

As both the women had young children in prams, they were relieved to see that at last something was being done to aid young mums with prams to cross the treacherous Gants Hill roundabout.

At the moment ramps are being constructed in the subway, which serves five of the six arms of the roundabout. The five ramps will enable pedestrians to cross the road in greater safety.

A spokesman for the Ministry of Transport, Mr. R. E. Sharp told MARKET "We have no proposals other than what is being carried out at the moment."

Mrs. Kiesner and Mrs. Landon both thought it was "about time something was done" about the menace.

Mr. G. W. Harwood, of Church Road, Newbury Park, said the ramps would doubtless be welcomed by mothers with prams and by elderly people, but added:

"I doubt if they will make any difference to the able-bodied, sprightly people who choose to ignore the subway entirely and risk life and limb. . ."

Nina Boutique Modele

THE WORD IS SPREADING FAST ....

After 15 years experience in MAYFAIR, NINA is now advising and dressing all the discerning women in 15 miles radius of her select boutique that holds a collection of DIFFERENT clothes.

1B Balfour Road, Ilford, Telephone Ilford 4526.

(opposite Ilford Station — b) the taxi rank)

Traffic problems were increasingly aired in the press as traffic became heavier and crossing the road became more hazardous. Campaigns for new pedestrian crossings and traffic calming continued through to the end of the twentieth century and beyond.

The 'swinging sixties' brought a rash of boutiques to Ilford.

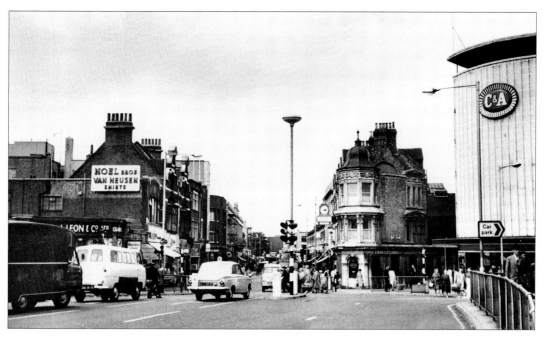

C&A's store opposite the station was a familiar sight on the corner of Ley Street during the last half of the century. It has now departed, to be replaced by a new Woolworths. Note the new-style street lamp and the sign directing motorists to a car park.

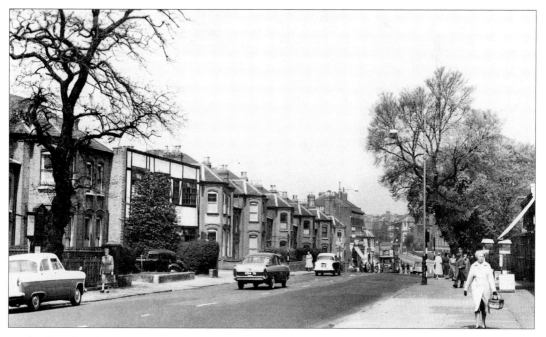

Cranbrook Road, with its more specialist shops. Many of the old houses on the left were converted into offices.

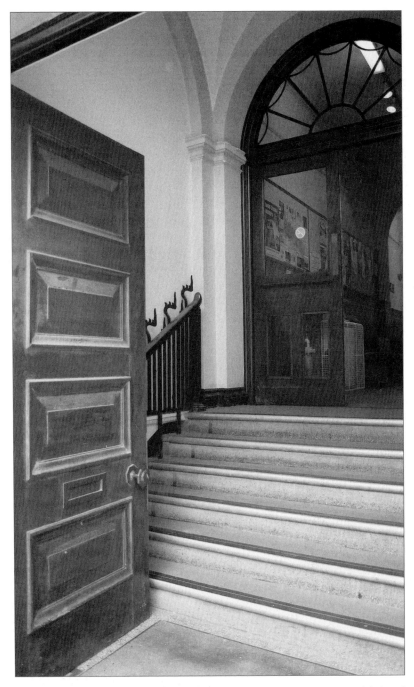

For much of the century this doorway led to the Central Library and the great delights of reading, learning and acquiring information. It was part of the side elevation of the town hall after the latter was extended in the early part of the twentieth century. The block is now used for other local government purposes.

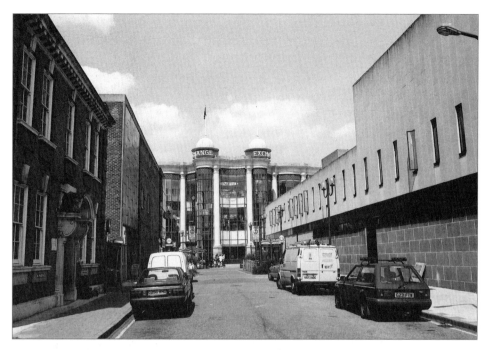

This is the High Road entrance to the Exchange shopping mall. To the right is the doorway that led up to the reference library premises after the war, before the new Central Library opened.

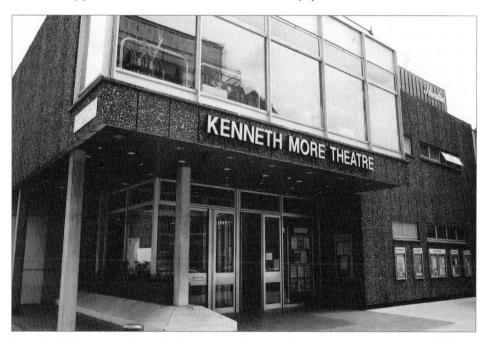

Opened in 1975 and named after the famous actor who presided at the topping-out ceremony in 1973, the theatre is a useful addition to Ilford's cultural life.

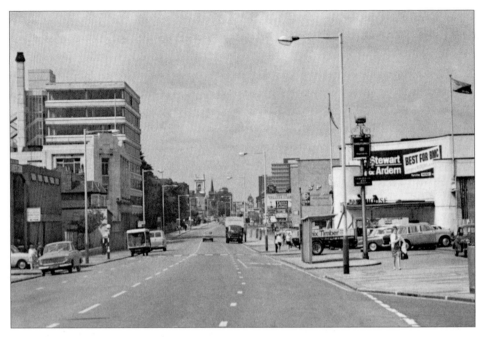

Viewed from the Cauliflower pub (just out of sight on the right), the buildings of new Ilford are beginning to soar upwards in the early 1970s.

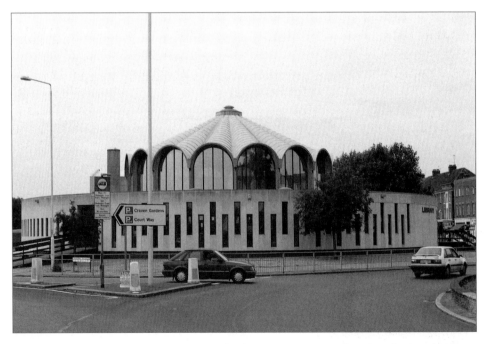

The Fulwell Cross Library was an innovative piece of architecture, moving away from the utilitarianism and new brutalism all around. It opened to the public in March 1968.

Centreway was a brave experiment which did not quite work. It was an early attempt at designing a small mall. The panel on the top of the corner shop at the entrance resembles an abstract design by Picasso.

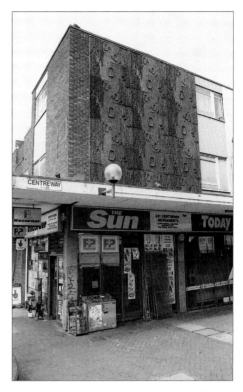

Looking into the interior of the disused part of the mall. Behind the boarded-off rear section, nature has reasserted itself, with large clumps of buddlejas growing freely. The staircase still leads to flats and to a car park at the rear.

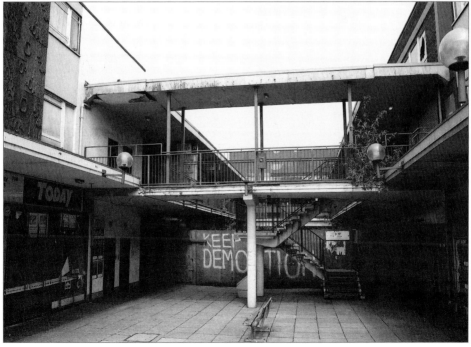

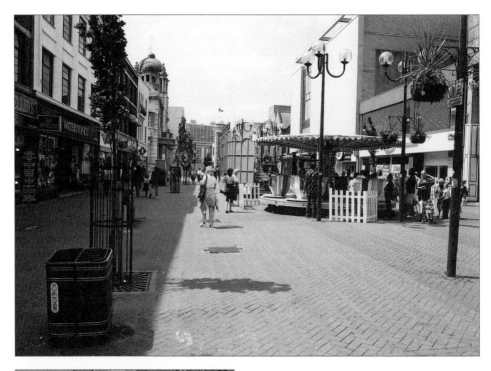

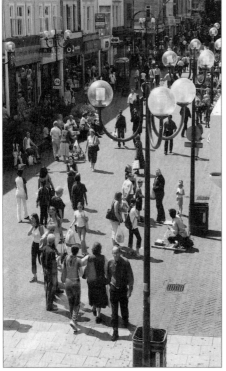

Pedestrianisation of the High Road towards the centre of Ilford has been very successful, creating an almost continental feel. The range and diversity of styles and continuing existence of some old buildings such as the town hall prevent the normal impression of modern sterility and give Ilford its own unique character.

Continental flair on the High Road, rescued from death by traffic.

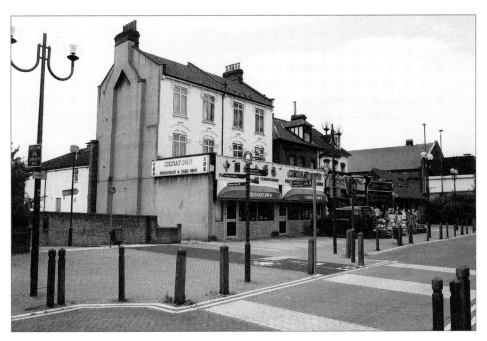

The eastward extension of the pedestrian scheme towards the new police station has formed another small plaza, and these older trading premises are in contrast with a new precinct on the other side. The hardware shop in the background still lays out a selection of its stock at the front in traditional Ilford fashion.

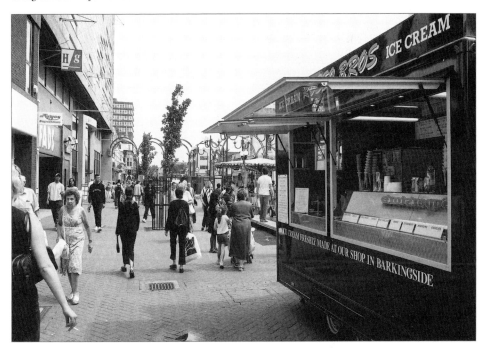

A fine day brings out the shoppers and the ice-cream booth by Harrison Gibson's.

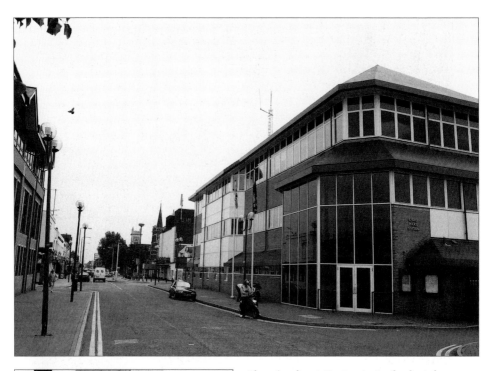

The new police station terminates the short plaza beyond the Griggs Approach overbridge.

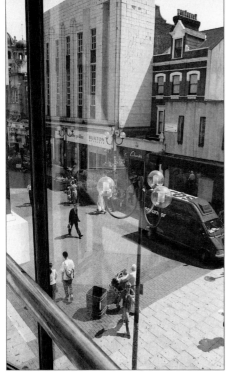

Contrasts from the Exchange windows. The white-tiled Burton's shop on the left was built in 1930, leaving a Victorian upper storey on either side. On the right the upper storey, a 1960s-style prefabricated structure, is overshadowed by both. The presence of the Securicor van on the pedestrian walkway spoils the freedom of the scene.

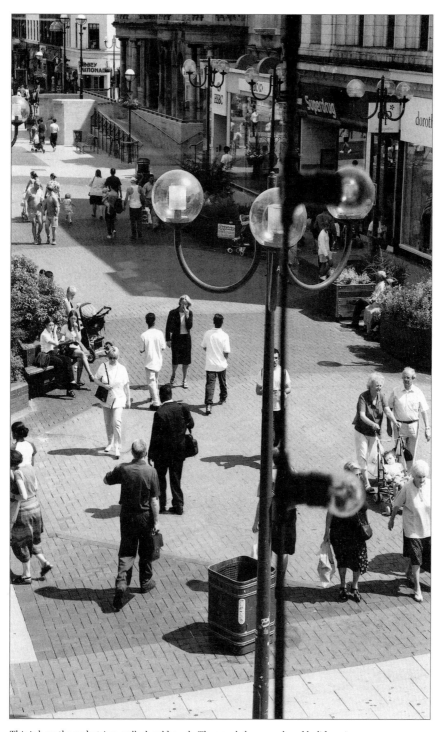

This is how the pedestrian walk should work. The people have a relaxed holiday air.

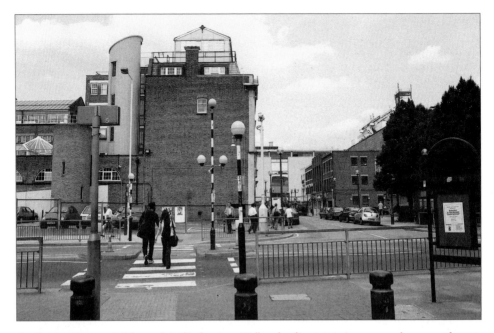

Another ingenious part of the modern Ilford system. Walkers heading into town come up from an underpass, avoiding the through road for traffic, and pass directly on to this pedestrian crossing by the new Central Library. Oakfield Road opposite takes them into the main centre of the High Road. The back of the town hall shows much individuality, with the hangar-like enclosure on the top and a modern 'periscope', presumably housing an emergency staircase. In addition, there is another round tower (like the bottom of a lighthouse), some semi-circular windows and an array of glass rooflights – tremendous fun as an architectural collection.

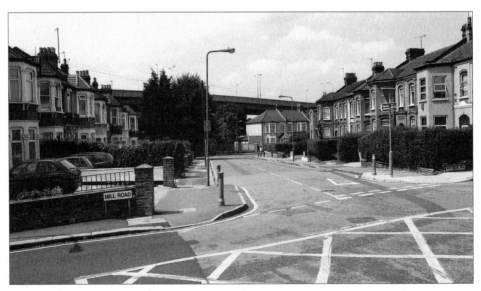

The typical houses of twentieth-century Ilford taper down to the Roding valley. It takes a moment to realise that the twenty-first-century Barking–Woodford Relief Road has been constructed beyond them along the valley. From a distance it looks like an old railway viaduct.

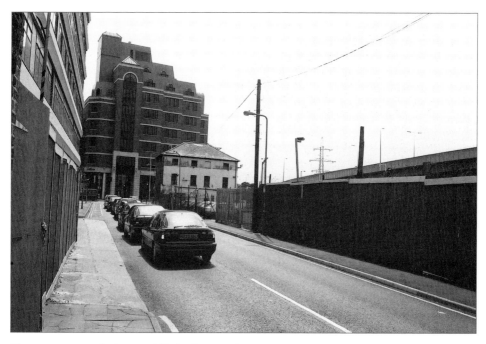

The new ziggurat at the bottom of Ilford Hill towers above a Victorian survivor clinging on to existence on this side of the hill, as seen from Mill Road. Over to the right is the line of the Barking–Woodford Relief Road.

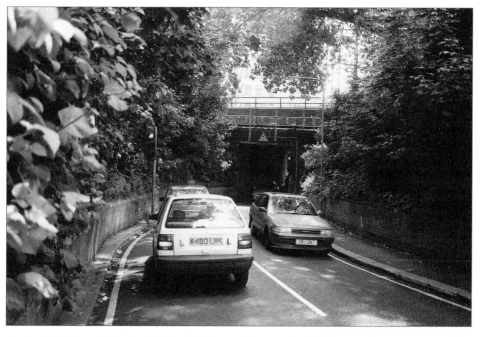

A relic of Ilford's past is 'the throat', where Mill Lane traffic queues for the lights controlling access through the single-lane tunnel under the railway.

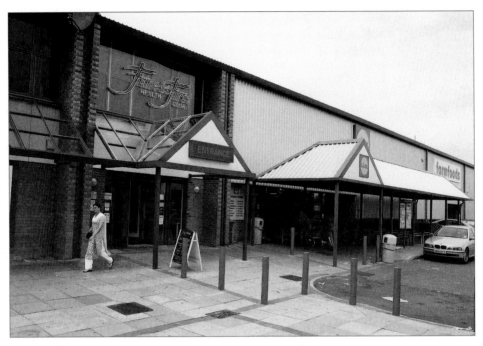

Thompson Close, a mini-precinct conveniently close to a large car park, a late arrival on the twentieth-century Ilford landscape near the railway tracks and depot. A health club and the supermarkets are all part of the 1990s scene.

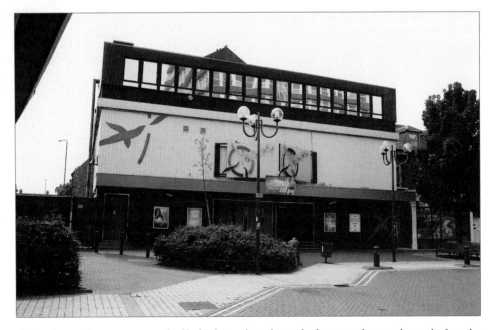

This modern music venue was once the Ilford Palais, a place of resort for dancers and extremely popular from the 1930s onwards. It was one of a chain around London.

The magic roundabout! This car park exit ramp with a pedestrian access-way underneath has a certain voluptuousness in its shape. The alley leading to this view comes from an opening in the High Road opposite the town hall. Turn around . . .

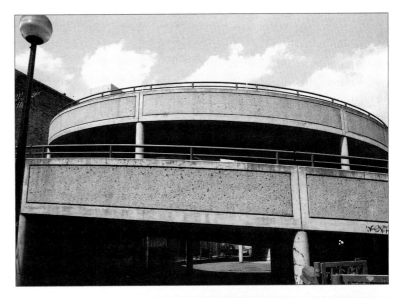

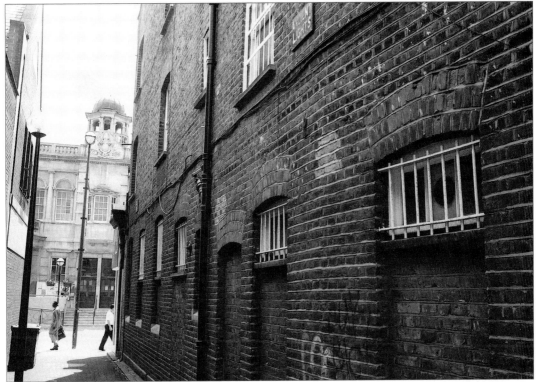

. . . and this is what you see. There's a wonderfully characterful piece of brickwork on the wall of the Victorian building with stopped-up doorway and blind and barred windows, but in addition there are two wooden boards bearing the inscription 'Ancient Lights'. At the beginning of the twentieth century there were many more of these, insisting on the prevention of any closer building or the blocking-out of precious daylight.

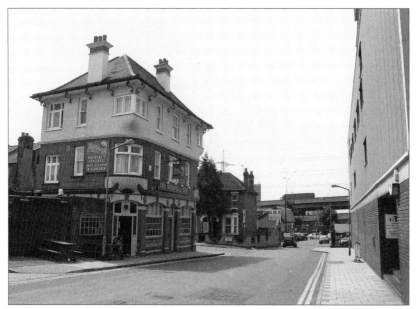

Looking for more clues to the past at the end of the twentieth century we come across the Sheepwalk Inn in Roden Street behind Sainsbury's and the one-way road system. For most of the twentieth century this inn was the Papermakers Arms, commemorating the old paper factory that once stood off Ilford Hill.

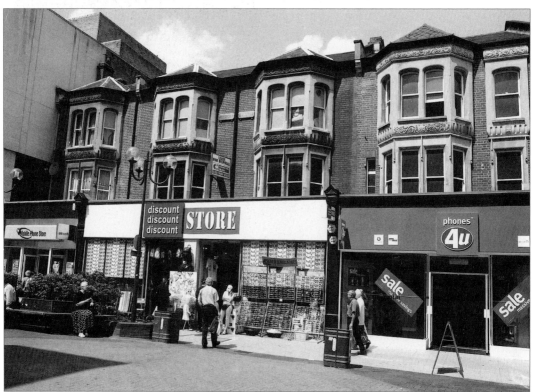

Look up in the High Road opposite the town hall and you can see the plaque indicating that these were the old *Ilford Recorder* offices and printing concern. The frontage also bears the Essex coat of arms and other small details.

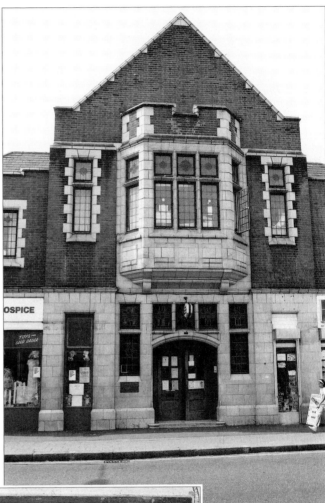

In Ilford Lane is the attractive 1930s-style frontage of the Methodist Hall. A plaque was placed here by Ilford Council to celebrate the Festival of Britain in 1951. The inscription points out that the site was once the Uphall brick-pits where the remains of animals of the Pleistocene age were found (known irreverently as the 'Ilford Elephants').

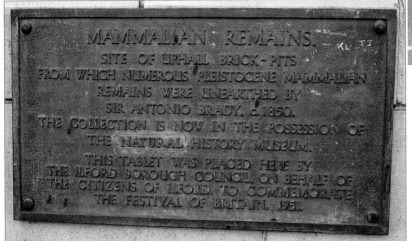

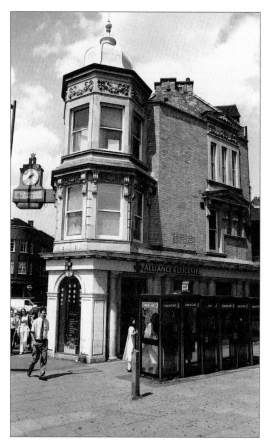

Two striking bank buildings. The Alliance & Leicester building, occupied in earlier decades by various different firms, appears on photographs throughout the century. The interesting clock was added in mid-century. Barclays Bank on the High Road stands out from its neighbours in the neo-classical style favoured in the 1920s and 1930s. The style befits a bank with its quiet dignity, an image too many banks have cast off. The High Road is all the better for its presence.

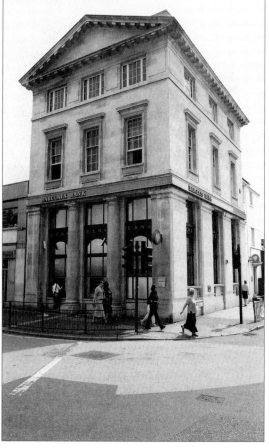

On Britannia Road we are surrounded by memories of the Ilford film works which lay behind these two cottages. The high pavement was intended to prevent flooding from the river nearby. The cottages make a nice contrast with the Sheepwalk on the corner.

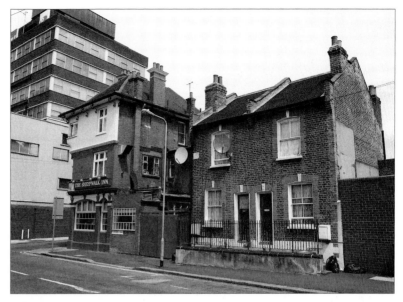

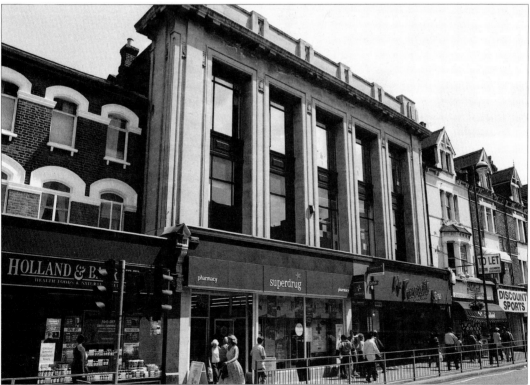

This striking frontage in Cranbrook Road was once the entrance to West's department store. Further along the road, occupying more modest premises, is the excellent local firm of Fairhead's, which has survived into the twenty-first century – one of only two businesses in this part of Cranbrook Road to do so (the other is Owen Clark).

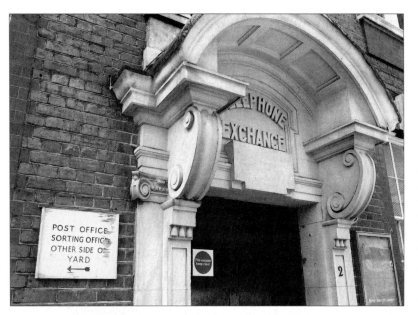

The old telephone exchange, situated on the corner of Postway Mews. Now redundant, it reminds us that telephones and mail services were once both under the aegis of the post office. The doorway is another one of the nice architectural details still to be found in central Ilford.

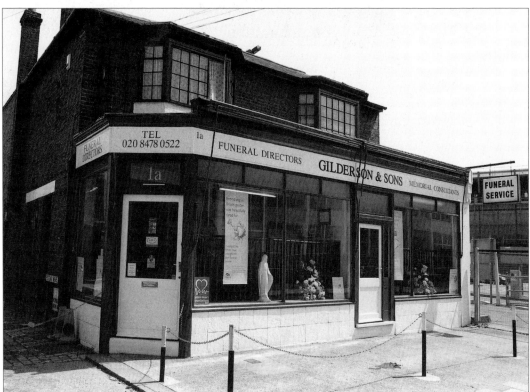

Gilderson's, opposite the exchange, is in a peaceful location, away from much of the bustle of the town. Below the premises, the old side road is cut in two by the new road system.

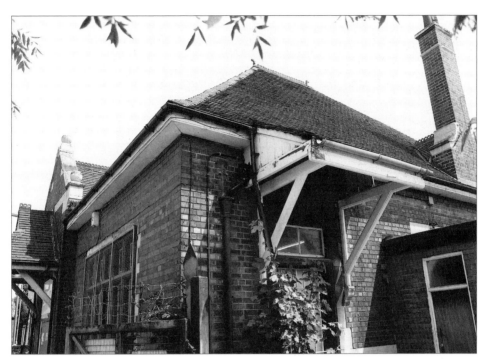

The second entrance to Ilford station, from York Mews and York Road, was partly paid for by builder Cameron Corbett to encourage prospective purchasers to buy his houses.

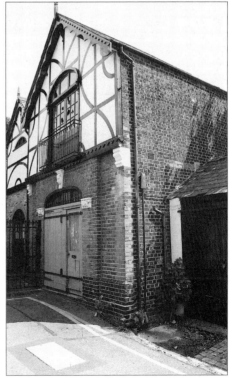

The original function of this building in York Mews is obscure. Was it a butcher's, or perhaps a builder's, or was it in fact stables?

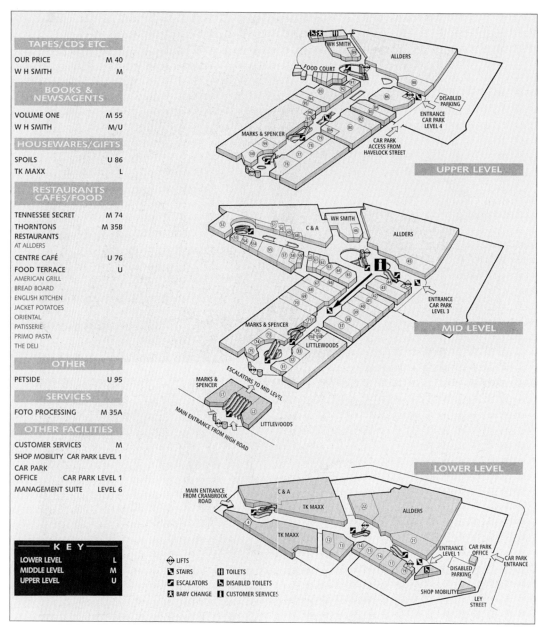

Early publicity and the plan for the Exchange shopping mall, which had an enormous impact on shopping in the town at the end of the twentieth century.

The left towers of the Exchange at the High Road end are given perspective by the greengrocer's stall across the road.

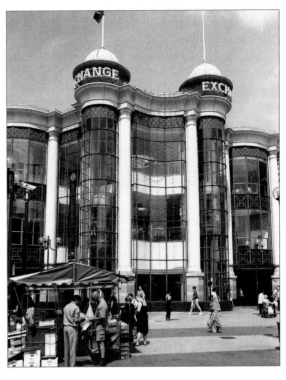

'In Xanadu a stately pleasure dome . . .' – the roof of the Exchange.

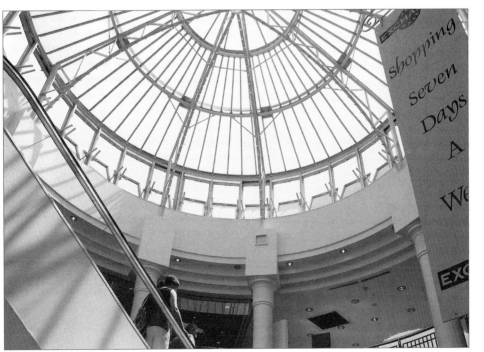

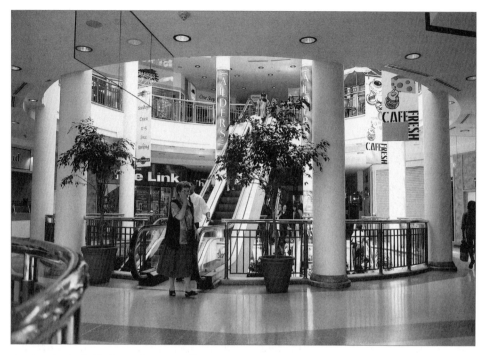

Another vista in the Exchange shopping mall.

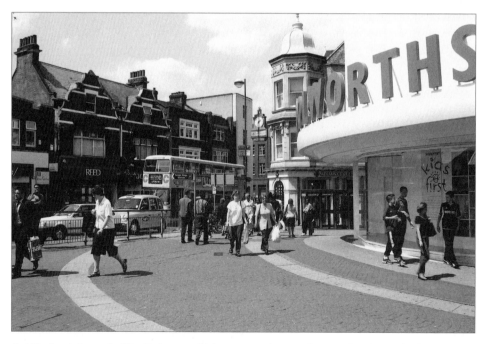

Outside the station end of the Exchange, which was once the exit of ancient Ley Street, the former site of C&A's is now occupied by Woolworths. It is now a Wilkinson's store.

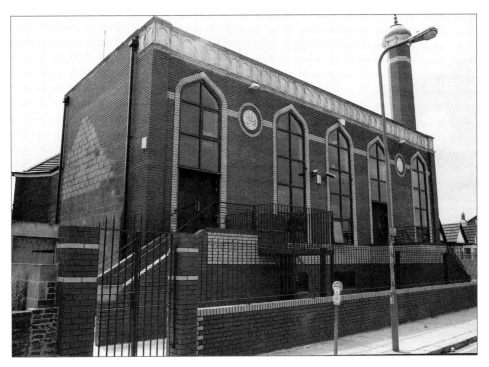

Exotic Ilford, where the muezzin cries! Ilford mosque
arrived at the end of the century.

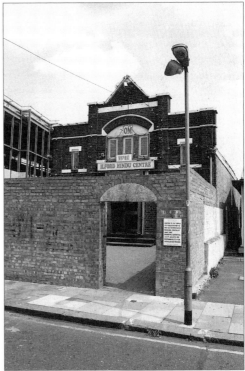

The Ilford Hindu Centre lies behind this wall and is
housed in an old chapel.

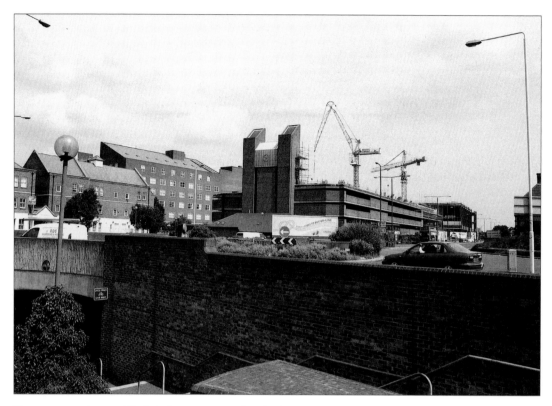

The new century has seen Ilford's built environment still restlessly growing. Cranes tower above the new works in the distance. This picture was taken from the corner of Ilford Lane, near the underpass.

Acknowledgements and Picture Credits

I would like to thank the following individuals and organisations for their help and support during the compilation of this book:

Bill Byers and the *Ilford Recorder*, page 86 bottom, page 96 bottom; Mr Tony Clark, pages 66–7; Mrs M. Gladding, pages 60 and 73; the Plessey Company, page 82 bottom.

Special thanks are due to Keith Langridge, who has made a major contribution with his outstanding photography of modern Ilford on pages 102–3, 104 bottom, 105–19, 121–4 and 126–7.

All remaining photographs are from the author's collection.

Barkingside Library

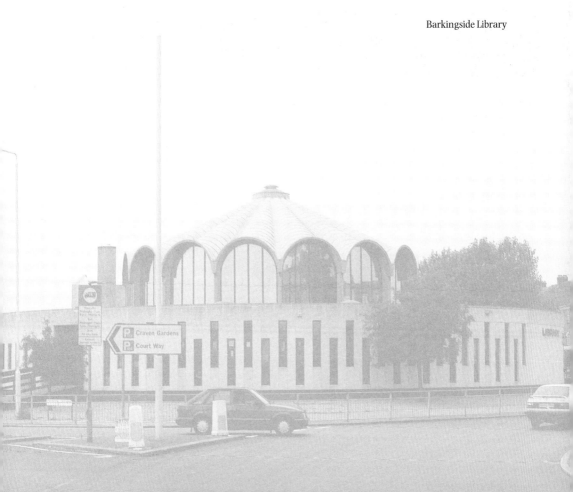

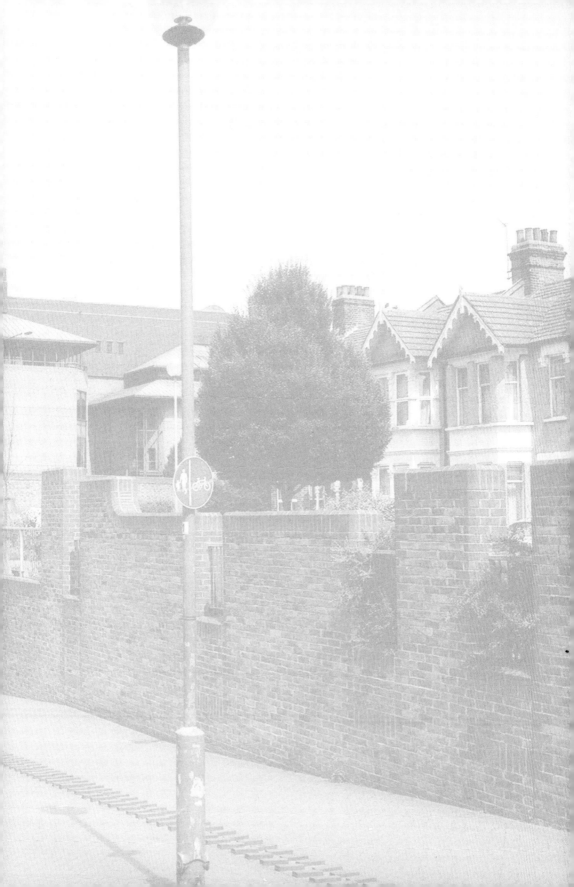